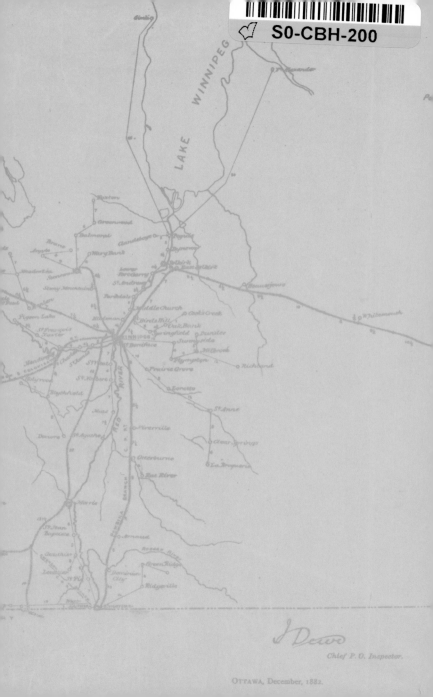

LAKE WINNIPEG

Ft. Alexander

Selkirk

East Selkirk

Winnipeg

St. Boniface

RED RIVER

Morris

J. Dewe

Chief P. O. Inspector.

OTTAWA, December, 1882.

Letters

from a young

emigrant

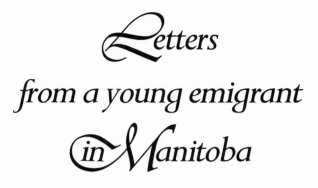

Letters
from a young emigrant
in Manitoba

Edited and with an Introduction
by Ronald A. Wells

The University of Manitoba Press

© The University of Manitoba Press 1981

Map on endpapers of Manitoba post offices courtesy
Public Archives of Canada.

Canadian Cataloguing in Publication Data

ffolkes, Edward.

Letters from a young emigrant in Manitoba

Attributed to Edward ffolkes. cf. Peel, 2nd ed., 675.
First published: London: K. Paul, Trench, 1883. ISBN 0-88755-126-2

1. ffolkes, Edward. 2. Frontier and pioneer life — Manitoba.
3. Manitoba — Emigration and immigration — Biography. I. Wells,
Ronald A. (Ronald Albert), 1941– II. Title.

FC3373.1.F49A3 1981 971.27'02'0924
~~F1063.F49A3 1981~~   C81-091100-0

36,200

Contents

Editor's Introduction   7

Preface   41

Introduction   43

The Letters   45

Acknowledgements

I WISH to express gratitude to Calvin College, and especially to its Dean, John Vanden Berg, both for encouragement and for financial assistance, which afforded me the opportunity to pursue various aspects of British migration to North America; to the Institute of United States Studies, University of London, where this and other work began; to the library staff of the British Museum; and to my wife Kathleen for all her assistance, both editorial and personal.

Ronald A. Wells
Calvin College

Editor's Introduction

IN 1883, the London publishing house of Kegan Paul,
Trench and Company brought out an anonymous little
volume entitled *Letters From a Young Emigrant in
Manitoba*. It was part of a burgeoning literature about
Canada which appeared in England at the end of the
nineteenth century. The author is Edward ffolkes, an
English emigrant from Norfolk who had studied agriculture at the Ontario Agricultural College in Guelph
before taking up farming in Manitoba. The letters of
ffolkes are among the best records of immigrant life in
the Canadian Northwest during the time of that area's
early development. The historical importance of the
letters can be best understood when they, like other
books about emigration, are viewed in the larger
context of, in this case, British emigration to North
America.

Maldwyn A. Jones, in an article on British migration in the nineteenth century, suggests future areas of research.[1] He changes the focus from the United States as the receiving country to Britain as the sending country, a focus which must embrace the several countries to which Britons migrated during the nineteenth century.[2] It would seem less productive to dwell unduly on assimilation in the receiving country, or even to use the terms "emigration" or "immigration." Rather, it is more useful for historical understanding to speak of "migration" and to investigate "the complete experience of migration from one society to another"—a migration which took place within an "Atlantic economy."[3]

In the past, students of migration have tended to emphasize the United States, the "distant magnet" which drew some forty million Europeans to its shores. Indeed, the plethora of scholarship on various aspects of the American story is understandable given the fact that, as Oscar Handlin has noted, "immigrants are American history."[4] But as Jones suggests, we know much less than we would like to know about why Europeans migrated. And, when scholars begin to study the European background to migration, they find that the United States assumes its proper place as merely one of many possible destinations for the potential migrant. For British migrants, Canada, New Zealand, and Australia were at least as important as the United

8

States, especially during the thirty-year period centred on the turn of the twentieth century.[5]

One of the most interesting questions about British migration is: why was there such a substantial switch in destination from the United States to Canada, beginning as early as the end of the nineteenth century, and why did the rate accelerate rapidly during the years before the First World War?[6]

I think that we must question the role of emigration agents in influencing choice of destination. Both before Confederation[7] and after, Canadian agents were only marginally successful in diverting the migration stream from the United States to Canada.[8] Yet when that stream, at least the one from Britain, did turn in Canada's favour, it "was as welcome as it was unexpected."[9] Government attempts to lure farmers from the United States to the Canadian Northwest, however, appear to have been more successful.[10] What drew Americans to the Canadian West was the same thing which drew Britons: the availability of good land, and, with the coming of the railway, Canadian land was commercially viable. It did not seem to matter whether or not agents were trying to lure migrants to the Canadian West; migrants came when it seemed that the promise of a better life was realistic. The Canadian West may have become more attractive to British migrants because of the "closing" of the American frontier, and because with its new cities, it offered urban as well as agricultural economic opportunities.[11]

A more plausible reason for the turning of the migratory stream to Canada is the development of heightened imperial consciousness after 1885. When Britain became the premier imperialist power in the world, many British migrants may have chosen Canada for patriotic reasons; this, coupled with the opening of the Canadian West, may have created a very potent force directing migrants to Canada. A widely read pamphlet of the period describes the situation as being precisely so: in *The Colonist at Home Again, or, Emigration not Expatriation,* the author delighted at being back again in Manitoba, where, as an emigrant, he still lived under the British flag and not as an expatriate to another country.[12] Another pamphleteer, J.G. Moore, echoed the imperial refrain. He urged migrants to go to Manitoba precisely because it was an English province: "Above your heads still will float the Union Jack of England, in your walks abroad, in your every labour, in your daily life, the same old language will meet your ear. English hands will grasp yours, and English hearts to be more ready there, perhaps, than here to show their sympathy in your disappointment."[13] This is what W.L. Morton observed when he noted that during the 1880s Manitoba had become, despite its ethnic diversity, a British and Canadian province.[14]

Another aspect of imperial consciousness in turning British migrants to Canada may also have been the desire of Britons to avoid the United States precisely because the so-called "new immigration" was beginning in America. The presence of increasing numbers of southern and eastern Europeans in the United States may have turned Britons to Canada for two reasons: the "new" immigrants limited the range of opportunities available to the British;[15] and, the racial attitudes of imperialist thought, based as they were on Social Darwinian assumptions, may have caused Anglo-Saxon migrants to want to avoid the "new" immigrants for the same reasons that Anglo-Saxons already in America found them "unacceptable" and sought to restrict migration from southern and eastern Europe. The sure foundation of cultural Anglo-Saxonism which John Fiske and Henry Cabot Lodge feared would be eroded in the United States if "new" immigrants continued to come, was precisely the foundation which pamphleteers, such as Moore and Pocock, could promise prospective British migrants to western Canada.[16]

The pattern of English predominance in western Canada, and especially Manitoba, was established by the influx of both agriculturalists and urban workers. Professor Morton believes that this newer pattern of settlement was largely due to the so-called "great agricultural depression" which began in England in the mid-1870s.[17] However, we know that the depression was selective, and for some sectors of British agriculture the depression was more apparent than real.[18] There were probably relatively few British agricul-

11

turalists who were literally pushed off the field and who then migrated directly to western Canada. Those pushed off the field often lacked the resources to migrate and to begin a new life on the Canadian prairie. More typically, the agriculturalists who migrated to western provinces such as Manitoba were still on the land in England, but found themselves potential casualties of economic change and social disruption. They were forced to leave not so much because of the immediate press of circumstances but because of their fear that remaining in England would cause them to lose what material possessions and hope for the future they already had.[19] The fear of a worsening position in England and the hope for a better future in Canada were prime forces in bringing a larger number of English migrants to Canada during the last years of the nineteenth century.[20]

While the foregoing comments do offer possible answers to the question of why British emigration turned from the United States to Canada at the end of the nineteenth century, I believe that the expansion of popular knowledge about Canada in Britain is an area which might fruitfully be explored. The connection between popular knowledge of a foreign country and migration to that country is not an easy one to ascertain. Historians of British migration to the United States often point to the approximately two hundred American travel accounts which were published in Britain in the quarter century before the Civil War. Surely, one thinks, the rise in British migration to the United States was related in some way to this publishing phenomenon. Yet, while Jones is correct in cautioning that such a causal relationship is easier to assert than to demonstrate, some recent content analyses of newspapers and pamphlets have begun to suggest that relationship.[21]

In looking at Canada, it may be easier to explore the notion that an increase in popular knowledge about the country was related to larger British migration. The increase in literacy in Britain in the latter part of the nineteenth century, combined with improvements in technology which made fast, cheap printing possible, brought a flood of mass-produced newspapers and inexpensive editions of books ranging from religious tracts to novels of romance and adventure. Travel books and emigration guides were no longer read only by the upper classes, but were very popular with all readers. With a far larger number of people possessing a minimum reading ability, and with editions of books and pamphlets selling for six pence or one shilling, it would seem that the vast redirection of British migrants to Canada may be correlated (given however much imprecision, be it admitted) with the explosion of popular knowledge about Canada in Britain after 1880.

The most effective written stimuli to migration were, of course, emigrant letters; they have been widely studied, and they deserve their status as the most important source for historians studying migration. The most notable studies of emigrant letters have been concerned with the migration to the United States of the Norwegians, the Dutch, the Welsh, and the English.[22] The most sophisticated of these studies is Charlotte Erickson's study about the English migration. She agrees with Maldwyn Jones, who distrusts Marcus Hansen's belief in the efficacy of guidebooks in stimulating migration to pre-Civil War America.[23] Yet, one of her more striking conclusions is that the letters are efficacious primarily during the first half of the century. In explaining the dearth of emigrant letters in the last half of the century, she suggests that "as the volume of emigration grew, the emigrating individual from any particular town or family became less extraordinary. His action was not so much in the nature of an adventure into the unknown." Also, as shipping and labour information became more widely distributed through the vehicles of popular culture, "the letters became increasingly superfluous."[24] Moreover, since the Canadian part of the British migration story occurred largely at the end of the century, we might tend to value more highly the growth of popular knowledge in stimulating migration. Of course, when letters from emigrants were available, they provide the most valuable information; it is precisely because Edward ffolkes' letters appeared during a time when popular knowledge was increasing and could corroborate their contents, that their value was increased.

A great expansion of popular knowledge about Canada, especially the West, occurred in Britain in the 1880s. Before this, there was an "appalling ignorance" in Europe concerning Canada, a fact which Canadian emigration agents complained of when explaining their failure to attract migrants.[25] Even in England, the "vast majority of rural people" knew little of Canada, whereas the United States was not only well known, but was "considered to be the most attractive country in the world."[26] The lack of knowledge about Canada before 1880 is corroborated by Mary Agnes Fitzgibbon, author of one of the period's best travel books. A letter posted to her from England carried her address and only Winnipeg, Manitoba, omitting Canada. The letter had gone to several places in France, as evidenced by the diverse postmarks. One postal official in France wrote on the letter, "Try Calcutta." Another person finally added, "Nouvelle Amérique." The letter eventually reached her in Winnipeg, via New York, some three months after its original posting![27] Before 1880, if Britons thought at all about Canada, it seems they thought of it as part of an undifferentiated continental entity called "America." Prospective migrants were drawn to North America for various reasons, and they were indifferent about whether or not they ended up north or south of the Great Lakes, a feeling which allowed a substantial mingling of the peoples of North America.[28]

This changed greatly after 1880 as Canada became better known in Britain and the stream of migration turned very markedly in Canada's favour. A score of books and pamphlets about the Canadian West was published in Britain during the eighties, and about half that number in the nineties, most of them focusing on Manitoba.[29] There are several types into which this literature could be categorized: (a) serious travellers and long-term settlers, both of whom must be regarded as the most reliable sources of information, and on whom prospective migrants often relied; (b) government agencies, and the railways, all of which had obvious vested interests in bringing migrants to the West; (c) holiday travellers who wanted to "do" parts of the USA and Canada in a short time and then write a "light" book about their experiences when they returned home. Prospective migrants must seldom have relied upon the picture-postcard vignettes of such books as Thomas Greenwood's *A Tour in the States and Canada: Out and Home in Six Weeks* (1883), and Lady Aberdeen's *Through Canada With a Kodak* (1893). We would be doing justice to the past if we chose to critically accept the books of serious travellers and long-term settlers, to accept with greater criticism and some cynicism the pamphlets of government agencies and the railways, and to ignore the "light" books of holiday travellers.

Among the serious books published during the eighties and nineties, twelve are worthy of note.[30] They are "unassuming and informative" and we can regard them as relatively trustworthy guides to understanding British popular knowledge about Canada.[31] However, the pamphlets published under the auspices of the Canadian Pacific Railway or the Government of Manitoba must be viewed more critically because these bodies were decidely interested in enticing British migrants to Manitoba and the West, a case which could be made in reasonably objective terms. The pamphlets were no doubt helpful in giving information such as travel data, addresses of authorities in Manitoba, and how to avoid being defrauded by unscrupulous people.[32] The principal weakness of such pamphlets was that they were published anonymously, and a reader could not independently verify the prejudices or biases which might have informed the writing. Two government-published pamphlets, however, overcame this weakness, since they were not anonymous, and the authors were known in England to be men of good judgement; these pamphlets, then, must be regarded as the best of the lot.[33]

Taken together, all of this popular literature not only provided prospective migrants with a great deal of useful information, but it also gave them some indication as to how to evaluate the plethora of information. We note in the writings of the serious travellers and long-term residents a questioning, even a disdain, for the information given by, and even the motivations of, government and railway advertisements and encouragements. Many writers attack the "scene painting" of other pamphlets in which the migrant is promised prosperity and status in a salubrious climate. J.P. Pocock wrote: "The Canadian Government will find that a zealous concern for the welfare of those who seek its shores must, in the long run, do far more to attract settlers than all the puffing exertions of agents, or the one-sided statements of pamphlets so freely circulated in the United Kingdom to secure this end."[34] Even W.F. Ray, in a government-published pamphlet, recognized that there were "many indiscreet eulogists" who were giving information which, because it promised too much to the migrant, would surely be counterproductive in the end. This sentiment was echoed by several other authors.[35] In fact, nearly all authors agreed that success in Manitoba and the West was ultimately possible for migrants who were hard working and who had not been influenced by unscrupulous agents.

Many of the books and pamphlets gave prospective migrants a great deal of practical information which was no doubt as welcome as it was useful. In

18

this connection, government and railway accounts were often as good as those published independently. A series of CPR pamphlets in the early nineties gave good advice on such wide-ranging practical matters as ocean and land travel, land laws, sales of government and privately held land, names and addresses of government officials in Manitoba, soil and climate conditions, and what clothes and equipment to bring.[36] The best of the CPR pamphlets, and surely the one calculated by the CPR to be received with trust by migrants seeking practical advice, was published a few years before the others. The pamphlet was entitled, *What Women Say of the Canadian North-West* (1886), and was the result of a CPR project which, in September, 1885, sent questionnaires to an unstated number of women in Manitoba. The introduction of the pamphlet states that the original replies to the questionnaire, from which the printed matter had been extracted, could be viewed at the CPR office in Cannon Street, London. The editor stated that unfavourable replies had not been deleted, and that giving a true picture of a settler's life in Manitoba was the CPR's only intention. Each woman was asked to answer a series of practical questions and to include her name and address. One of the questions was, "Shall the family accompany the intending settlers?" Mrs. J.D. Hanson of Turtle Mountain replied that it very much depended on the means and prior experiences of the

19

settlers. For example, a man with little capital and with small children and a wife unaccustomed to farm work would do better to move alone and send for his family once the initial problems of settlement had been solved. On the other hand, if a man had enough capital to begin farming immediately, and if his wife and children were willing and able to work with him, then they would do better to come together so that the family could experience all aspects of their new life together.[37] As to the questions of what difficulties might await the new settlers, all respondents admitted that at first the work was hard, unrewarding, and lonely, but also that the attitude which the settler brought to his new life was the crucial matter determining his ultimate success or failure, a sentiment expressed by Mrs. J.P. Alexander of Sourisford and echoed by Mrs. S.J. Batcock of Orange Ridge.[38] The respondents advised newcomers to leave all bulky items behind, especially furniture, but to bring along a sewing machine, warm and practical clothing, and vegetable and flower seeds. They also gave some philosophical advice: Mrs. P.W. Davis of Chater wrote, "Do not come thinking to have a fortune in a year or so....Too many come expecting to commence here just where they left off in some other country.... But come determined that, with the blessing of God, you will have a home for yourself and children, and do not be above work, but rather willing to turn your hand to any respectable work that may present itself, and there is sure success."[39] Mrs. Clementina Livingstone of Lake Francis replied more critically: "My advice to intending emigrants is that of *Punch* to bachelors about to marry — 'don't.' If they are to come, my advice is first beware of those interesting works of fiction, the Government pamphlets."[40] On the question of climate, nearly all of the 82 respondents pronounced it healthy for both adults and children, some even suggesting its curative qualities for those who had suffered from respiratory ailments in Britain. Mrs. J.C. Sturgeon of Stockton went even further in extolling the salubrity of Manitoba's climate, noting that "three doctors at different times have failed to make a living in our district."[41]

The most practical of all questions for Britons thinking of farming in Manitoba or the Northwest was: "How much money did one need to get a proper start?" In the early 1880s there was agreement among the writers that one needed between £100 and £150 ($500–$750, at the then-current exchange rate of approximately 1:5). Thomas Moore stated that in 1879 one could get minimally underway in Manitoba for £100, noting that if one wanted an improved farm in a settled district in Ontario, the figure would have to be several times that. W.F. Ray agreed in 1880 that the difficulties and disadvantages of pioneer life could be initiated with a £100 stake.[42] In 1882 and

1885, writers suggested that the minimum stake had risen to £150.[43] By 1892, P.R. Ritchie observed that the minimum starting-up amount had risen to £200 ($1,000); this was confirmed by W.M. Elkington in 1895, who gave a very detailed breakdown of precisely what the initial costs would be.[44]

Finally, another theme in all of these popular books and pamphlets was the movement away from a North American consciousness to an imperial consciousness. In the early 1880s a North American consciousness still existed, in which it was possible to refer to the West in the undifferentiated term "America." As late as 1881, W.F. Munro, a twenty-year resident of Ontario and Manitoba, could write of the relative meaninglessness of the border:

> The great plain contained within the limits of the Province of Manitoba is perhaps less than one-half of the entire [Red River] valley; the other half, thanks to Lord Ashburton, forms part of the far extending possessions of Uncle Sam. His share is much larger, but not so wide; in every other respect it is much the same — the same climate, soil and productions; the people are the same; they live in the same way and for the same purpose — that is, to grow wheat. An imaginary line divides them; that is all.[45]

By 1884, C.C. Prance could still entitle his book *Notes on America,* even though the portion of his trip spent in the United States was only from New York to Montreal. However, we see the beginnings of the change in Prance's suggestion that Canada was a more suitable field for emigrating Englishmen than was the United States.[46]

In 1882, the "retired officer" (noted above as either Pocock or Goodridge) wrote of the superior advantages of Manitoba and the Northwest Provinces of British North America to the United States, but there was nothing up to then so strident as his 1889 writing in which he described residence in Canada as "emigration," and residence in the United States as "expatriation."[47] In 1883, J.C. Moore was already delighting in the fact that Manitoba was a British province.[48] Early in the twentieth century, as the imperial consciousness grew, this feeling could be described in quite chauvanistic terms, such as in the romantic novels of E.A. Wharton Gill, whose books were popular in England. In *A Manitoba Chore Boy,* Gill, who was canon of St. John's Cathedral, Winnipeg, presents a version of a Horatio Alger story in which young Tom Lester got ahead with "pluck and luck," but, of course in an irreducibly British–Canadian way.[49] The final apotheosis of the "Britishness" of Manitoba and the Northwest comes in a pamphlet published and circulated in Britain by the Manitoba Department of Agriculture and Immigration. The official view which Manitoba had of itself, of course, held out an invitation to Britons "to accept a share of Manitoba's prosperity ... in the firm belief that nowhere are the opportunities greater, the soil richer, the climate more healthy." All this was promised, and 160 free acres, "in a country where British traditions are upheld and where British law and justice hold sway."[50]

Even if we accept a cautious approach in demonstrating the connection between migration to, and popular knowledge of, Canada, we as historians might well consider the evidence in this literature and pay closer attention to the important question of why British migration turned in Canada's favour at the end of the nineteenth century.

It has been suggested that Edward ffolkes' *Letters From a Young Emigrant in Manitoba* is among the best records of Canadian immigrant life.[51] The title of the book is somewhat misleading, since more than one-third of the letters were written from Guelph, Ontario, while Edward was a student at the Ontario Agricultural College. Less is known about Edward ffolkes than one would like, but we do know enough to be confident about the veracity of his letters, and to assign him a place in the front rank of "ordinary" citizens whose writings reveal a great deal about life in western Canada at the end of the nineteenth century.

Edward ffolkes was the second son of Reverend Henry ffolkes, Church of England rector of Hillington, Norfolk, England.[52] The letters, written between 7 October 1880 and 23 September 1882, were brought to publication by the boy's mother, who wrote an introduction from the rectory in Hillington, and by her brother, Edward's uncle, Charles Hugh Everard, a classics master at Eton College, Windsor, from 1872 to 1893.[53]

Even though the last published letter is dated 23 September, Edward's mother and uncle must have decided on publication well before that — her introduction is dated 20 August 1882 and his is dated October 1882. "Uncle Charlie," as Edward referred to his uncle, began his introduction by stating that these letters were written from "America."[54] This, of course, was common parlance in the early 1880s when western Canada had not yet been undifferentiated from the United States in the minds of many people in England. Ted, as he referred to himself, apparently thought that his diary would someday become public; he told his mother that he would "always send the diary separate from the letters, so that you may show it to whoever is interested in my welfare."[55] This also conforms to standard usage at the time, in that many semi-public letters were later collected and published if they were thought valuable enough to future migrants, especially if they contained verifiable, practical information.

At college in Guelph, ffolkes had a good time socially and he enjoyed both the academic and practical aspects of his training. However, the practical training was a severe testing. His brother, Frank, was apparently thinking of emigrating, and Ted wrote,

"...tell Frank for me, to strain every nerve, to work for what he is trying for; that if emigration is the alternative, it is better to live in England with almost nothing than farm in Canada and be rich (if rich he ever can be)."[56] Several weeks later he seems to have passed through the depression caused by fatigue and was now ready to move west. In the spirit of North American culture, in which achievement could be measured most easily in monetary terms, he wrote, "I am beginning to have some confidence in myself.... I am my own tutor, but my purse, this time five years, will be my examiner, and dollars and cents will represent the marks I have made in the preliminary."[57]

Ted's first letter from Manitoba, written on 23 November 1881, revealed how tough he was and how ready he was to begin his new life. Writing from Cyprus Lodge, some thirty miles south of Portage la Prairie, he reported on his more-than-three-day journey from Toronto in which he and his companions were stranded for a night in a remote area because of track difficulties, and said that they remained tolerably warm only by burning the pieces of platform which they had torn up. Upon leaving Emerson, Manitoba, he developed a case of frostbite. Nevertheless, this first letter ends with a declaration of his future plans to buy a farm and a tentative request for money to buy it. He already found himself agreeing with the statement that, "He who tastes Red River water always returns."[58]

26

He spent his first months in the home of Graham Boulton, from whom he got good advice about purchasing land and about Manitoba farming in general. Also, the Boultons, a Plymouth Brethren family, provided a religious atmosphere at home which Ted appreciated very much.[59] In laying out plans for his future, he shows his healthy sense of humour by describing his loneliness as a bachelor on the frontier. He thought that many of his problems would be solved if he were to marry "some young lady well versed in scrubbing, washing, baking, dairying, getting up at 3:30 in summer, 5:30 in winter; strong nerves, strong constitution, obedient, and with money. Where can I find the paragon?"[60] We do not know whether or not Agnes Strachan, whom Ted later married, fitted such a description, but the evidence appears not to be so — the couple moved back to Ontario in a few years.

By the end of December, 1881, Ted had made enough local inquiries so that he could write to his parents asking for money to start farming on his own. He gave a detailed breakdown of possible expenses, concluding that £200 ($1,000) would get him started. This figure is somewhat higher than what other writers at the time had given, but they had given estimates for only the barest necessities. He noted that 1881 was the best time to buy land because the trains were bringing new migrants daily, and that an investment would pay off handsomely in a few years.[61]

During the early winter of 1882 he had stated his plans several times, with many variations, to his parents, in each case requesting their financial support. He reported having plans for several farms, and in February his detailed accounting for a relatively developed farm had risen to nearly £600 ($2,972).[62] Several options fell through, partly, he suggested, because land agents had been bribed by other men. By mid-March he rejoiced in receiving a letter from home which confirmed that the requestd £600 was on the way. He had purchased a 360-acre farm near Beaconsfield for $2,150 (£430), a good price for an improved farm. By late April he was busily at work at "Shore Lake Farm," and had already contracted for a labourer.[63] In late spring he already had his eye on more property, which, had he obtained it, would have been obtained "through a combination of consumate cheek (a thing a fellow must have in this country) and luck."[64] Ted seems to have possessed both, because his property soon measured two miles long and half a mile broad.

Ted's ambition was an engine which knew no rest, and his visions were as expansive as the Manitoba horizon. In mid-summer he wrote, like a character from a Horatio Alger story, that his daily routine was: "work, and sleep, eat, and work...on the dead run the whole time; and every now and then I look round and imagine I see a saw and grist mill looming up on the hill, at the border of the lake...the earlier a man begins, the earlier he wins, and I am afraid some-one else will get ahead of me if I don't look sharp...."[65] Not many farmers could have got ahead of Ted ffolkes who had his wheat harvested by 23 September, and was awaiting the components of his saw mill to arrive. With some satisfaction he could conclude his letters as follows: "Believing that I had performed all impera-tive duties, and resting in innocent security, I have thoroughly enjoyed my pipe every evening after tea, and then turned to bed, after thanking God for the bountiful blessings He has bestowed upon me, the magnificent weather He has given, and the abundant harvest, and the splendid health and spirits I at present possess to aid me in securing it."[66]

The book concluded with an epilogue written by his uncle, Charles Hugh Everard. Ted's uncle obviously delighted in the success of a lad of eighteen who had left England "with no experience and no advantages beyond average health and strength, and the courage and determination which are characteristics of English-men." However, he does concede that Ted's early success was dependent upon the considerable advant-age of having had £1,000 ($5,000) sent from England. Even so, it took considerable effort to turn that money into a prospering farm of 700 acres and the proposed saw and grist mills. But there was, according to Everard, more to Ted's success than could be measured "from the merely worldly point of view" (even though Ted himself had suggested that profit would be the gauge of his success). "No," said Everard, "the emigrant's career need not be only a continual hunt after the almighty dollar," as Ted's career also showed. His success was, in no small measure, due to the kindness and helpfulness which he was accorded by British–Canadians. Ted had grown personally, had developed "the better side of his nature," and it was because this "lesson" was evident in the letters that the uncle felt justified in publishing them."[67]

Not much else is known of Edward ffolkes' life. We know that he may have spent some time in British Columbia. His marriage to Agnes Strachan in 1891 preceded his return to Toronto in 1895. He was manager of the Wilkinson Plough Company and later manager of the Home Smith and Company's Humber Valley property. He died on 1 April 1916, at the age of 54, by accidental drowning in the Humber River, while helping Bell Telephone linemen repair damages which had occurred during spring flooding.[68]

While one would like to know more about the life of Edward ffolkes, more knowledge would be largely beside the point of our present interest in him. ffolkes is interesting because his letters are among the best examples of the genre of emigration literature which began to appear at the end of the nineteenth century. His story is a personal one, and the letters he wrote may well have spoken volumes to those in England who were contemplating migration. We might recall in this connection what Theodore C. Blegen has written about emigration letters and the worth of studying an individual's response to migration. Even though Blegen's comments are in terms of Norwegians writing home from the United States, the comments seem equally valid for Englishmen writing home from Canada:

> The immigrant's image of America, portrayed with a thousand details in letters, is interesting not only as a record of what was thus transmitted directly to vast numbers of people in Europe in the nineteenth century, but also a propelling force in emigration itself. There has been all too often an air of impersonality in accounts of American immigration. The coming of thirty millions of people was a movement of such magnitude that, to many, it has seemed futile to try to disengage personalities from the mass. Many writers have forgotten the individual man in the surging complex of international circumstances. World forces pushed people out of their accustomed environment; world forces pulled them westward with magnetic power. But the pivot of human motion is individual life. Migration was a simple individual act — a decision that led to consequences — and the "American letters" were a dynamic factor, perhaps the most effective single factor in bringing discontent to a focus and into action.[69]

We know less than we would like to know about why Europeans migrated to North America. Even considering the substantial social dislocation Europeans suffered at home, we have not yet been clearly able "to identify the circumstances in which men opted

31

for the most drastic of the available alternatives." But we do recognize that the motivations for migration are very complex indeed.[70] If it is true that an increase in British popular knowledge of Canada was a factor among the many reasons for British migration to Canada, and if emigrant letters are one of the key sources, then the letters of Edward ffolkes deserve to be read and studied. If Allan Nevins could suggest that the writings of British travellers in the United States were "among the most vital records of [the American] national past,"[71] then I would also suggest that, for the social history of Canada, Edward ffolkes' *Letters From a Young Emigrant in Manitoba* is among the vital records of the Canadian national past.

[1] Maldwyn A. Jones, "The Background to Emigration From Great Britain in the Nineteenth Century," *Perspectives in American History,* VII (1973), 3-92.

[2] Frank Thistlethwaite, "Migration From Europe Overseas in the Nineteenth and Twentieth Centuries," *Rapports de XIe Congrés International des Sciences Historique* (Stockholm, 1960), V, 32-60.

[3] *Ibid.,* 57; Carlton G. Qualey, "Immigration, Emigration, Migration," in O.F. Ander (ed.), *In the Trek of the Immigrants* (Rock Island, Ill., 1964), 33-38; Brinley Thomas, *Migration and Economic Growth: A Study of Great Britain and the Atlantic Economy* (Cambridge, 1953).

[4] Oscar Handlin, *The Uprooted* (Boston, 1951), 3.

[5] N.H. Carrier and J.R. Jeffery, *External Migration: A Study of the Available Statistics* (London, 1953).

[6]Between the years 1896 and 1914 the percentage of the total number of immigrants from Britain who settled in Canada rose from 9.5 to 47.0, while the percentage of the total number of immigrants from Britain who settled in the United States dropped from 66.0 to 24.7. Source: Walter Willcox, ed., *International Migrations,* 2 vols. (New York: National Bureau of Economic Research, 1929).

[7]Paul W. Gates, "Official Encouragement of Immigration by the Province of Canada," *Canadian Historical Review,* XV (March, 1934), 24-38.

[8]Norman Macdonald, *Canada, Immigration and Colonization* (Aberdeen, 1966), esp. 38ff.

[9]*Ibid.,* 38.

[10]Harold Troper, *Only Farmers Need Apply* (Toronto, 1972).

[11]Jones, "Background to Emigration From Great Britain," 75-77.

[12](London and Montreal, 1889). Like many other Victorian pamphleteers the author remained anonymous. Professor W.L. Morton believes the author to have been a Captain Goodridge. *Manitoba: A History* (Toronto, 1957), 493. However, the same man also wrote, *A Year in Manitoba, Being the Experiences of a Retired Officer in Settling His Sons* (London and Edinburgh, 1882), and Norah Story names him as J.P. Pocock. See *Oxford Companion to Canadian History and Literature* (London, 1967), 509.

[13]*Fifteen Months Round About Manitoba* (London, 1883), 28.

[14]Morton, *Manitoba,* 234-50.

[15]Jones, "Background to Emigration From Great Britain," 76-77.

[16]"The Anglo-Saxon Complex" is described well in Barbara W. Solomon, *Ancestors and Immigrants* (Chicago, 1972),

59-81. A recent book which illumines well the English-speaking, protestant nature of expansion to the Canadian West is: Doug Owram, *Promise of Eden: The Canadian Expansion Movement and the Idea of the West,* 1856–1900 (Toronto, 1980).

[17] Morton, *Manitoba,* 177ff.

[18] T.W. Fletcher, "The Great Depression of English Agriculture, 1873–1896," *Ecomomic History Review* (Second Series), XII (April, 1961), 417-31.

[19] Jones, "Background to Emigration From Great Britain," 90.

[20] Several authors found many farmers in Manitoba who had left agricultural pursuits in England for fear of losing what little money and status they had left. See especially Thomas Moore, *A Tour Through Canada in 1879* (London, 1880), 45; S.J. Pocock, *Across the Prairie Lands of Manitoba and the Canadian North-West* (London, 1882), p. 54.

[21] Jones, "The Background to Emigration from Great Britain," 18-19. Ronald A. Wells, "The Voice of Empire: *The Daily Mail* and British Migration to North America," *The Historian* XLII (February, 1981), 240-57. William E. Van Vugt, "English Emigrant Guidebooks and Pamphlets, 1860–1899: The Image of America," unpublished M.A. thesis, Department of History, Kent State University, 1981.

[22] Theodore C. Blegen, *Land of Their Choice, The Immigrants Write Home* (Minneapolis, 1955); Henry S. Lucas, *Dutch Immigrant Memoirs and Related Writings* (Assen, Netherlands, 1955); Alan Conway, *The Welsh in America, Letters from the Immigrants* (Minneapolis, 1961); Charlotte J. Erickson, *Invisible Immigrants: The Adaptation of English and Scottish Immigrants in Nineteenth Century America* (Coral Gables, Florida and London, 1972).

[23] Hansen, *The Atlantic Migration* (New York [Torchbook edition], 1961), 150; Erickson, *Invisible Immigrants,* 32-33, 491.

[24] Erickson, *Invisible Immigrants,* 231.

[25] Macdonald, *Immigration and Colonization,* 33.

[26] Quoted in *ibid.*

[27] *A Trip to Manitoba* (London, 1880), 58-59.

[28] Gerald M. Craig (ed.), *Early Travellers in the Canadas* (Toronto, 1955), xxx; Marcus Hansen and John Brebner, *The Mingling of the Canadian and American Peoples* (New Haven, 1940).

[29] An easily accessible review of some of the literature is in Elizabeth Waterston, "Travel Literature, 1880–1920," in Carl F. Klinck (ed.), *Literary History of Canada* (Toronto, 1965), 347-63; Norah Story (ed.), *Oxford Companion,* esp. 508-10.

[30] Thomas Moore, *A Tour Through Canada in 1879* (Dublin, 1880); W.F. Munro, *The Backwoods of Ontario and the Prairies of the North-West* (London, 1881); Sidney J. Pocock, *Across the Prairie Lands of Manitoba and the Canadian North-West* (London, 1882); J. P. Pocock (or, Captain Goodridge) *A Year in Manitoba* (London, 1882); J.G. Moore, *Fifteen Months Round About Manitoba* (London, 1883); Edward ffolkes, *Letters* (1883); W. Henry Barneby, *Life and Labour in the Far, Far West* (London, 1884); Mary Georgina Hall, *A Lady's Life on a Farm in Manitoba* (London, 1884); Courtaney C. Prance, *Notes on America* (Evesham, 1884); Anon., *Emigrant's Progress in Manitoba* (London, 1885); J.P. Pocock (or, Captain Goodridge), *The Colonist at Home Again* (London, 1889); W.M. Elkington, *Five Years in Canada* (London, 1895).

[31] Waterston, "Travel Literature," 348.

[32] The Canadian Pacific Railway pamphlets which enjoyed some circulation in England are: *What Women Say of the Canadian North-West* (London, 1886); *The Canadian North-West: What Farmers Say* (London, 1891); *The North-West*

Farmer in Manitoba, Assiniboia and Alberta (Liverpool, 1891); *Free Homes in Manitoba* (London, 1892). Government pamphlets Include: *Why Not Go to Manitoba?* (London, 1892); *Manitoba, Opinions of Eminent Men* (London, 1893).

33 W. Fraser Ray, a distinguished reporter for the *London Times,* was sent to Canada in 1878 and 1880. His dispatches later were reprinted as *Newfoundland to Manitoba: A Guide Through Canada's Maritime, Mining and Prairie Provinces* (London, 1881), which sold at six shillings. The Manitoba Government reprinted only the section about the province as *Facts About Manitoba* (London, 1882) in a one-shilling edition which had a wide circulation. P.R. Ritchie, an Essex farmer, toured the Canadian West independently in 1892. His report was favourable enough to encourage the government in Ottawa to reprint it as *Manitoba and the North-West Territories* (Ottawa, 1892), and to circulate it in Britain.

34 *A Year in Manitoba,* 27.

35 *Facts About Manitoba,* 43; *Emigrants Progress in Manitoba,* 1-2; Elkington, *Five Years in Canada,* 5.

36 *What Farmers Say* (1891), *Farming and Ranching in Western Canada* (1891), *The North-West Farmer* (1891).

37 *What Women Say,* 4.

38 *Ibid.,* 6.

39 *Ibid.,* 11.

40 *Ibid.,* 12.

41 *Ibid.,* 19.

42 Moore, *Tour Through Canada,* 39; Ray, *Facts About Manitoba,* 57.

43 *A Year in Manitoba,* 90; *Emigrants Progress in Manitoba,* 6.

44 *Manitoba and the North-West Territories,* 49; *Five Years in Canada,* 135.

45 *The Backwoods of Ontario,* 69.

46 *Notes on America,* 35.

47 *A Year in Manitoba,* 101; *The Colonist At Home Again,* 160.

48 *Fifteen Months Round Manitoba,* 28.

49 Published in London by the Religious Tract Society (1912), the book was published in two editions. Gill's two other books, *Love in Manitoba* (London, 1911), and *An Irishman's Luck* (London, 1914) were similarly saccharin versions of life, labour and love in British North America.

50 *Manitoba: The First Province of Canada* (1916).

51 Story, *The Oxford Companion to Canadian History and Literature,* 509.

52 L.R. Benson, "An O.A.C. Student in the 1880's," *Ontario History,* XLII (April, 1950), 67; *Crockford's Clerical Directory* (London, 1882), 368.

53 For help in tracing the family I am indebted to Mary Pearce, formerly of the British Museum, and to Jeremy Potter, librarian at Eton College.

54 *Letters,* v.

55 *Ibid.,* 11.

56 *Ibid.,* 55.

57 *Ibid.,* 60-61.

58 *Ibid.,* 75.

59 *Ibid.,* 82.

60 *Ibid.,* 90.

61 *Ibid.,* 97-98.

62 *Ibid.,* 130.

63 *Ibid.,* 140.

64 *Ibid.*, 143.

65 *Ibid.*, 158.

66 *Ibid.*, 170.

67 *Ibid.*, 177-81.

68 Benson, "An O.A.C. Student," 79.

69 *Land of Their Choice,* 7.

70 Jones, "Background to Emigration From Great Britain," 92.

71 *America Through British Eyes* (New York, 1948), 341.

Letters

from a young

emigrant

Preface

THIS little book consists of letters written from America by a young emigrant, giving an account of the first two years of his life, with a short introduction by his parents, with whose permission they are published. They are printed exactly as they were written, except that a few details, which could have no interest for the outside reader, are omitted, and that a name is occasionally changed. If the chance of their being useful to other young Englishmen, who may be thinking of following a like career, is not a valid pretext for their publication, I can only plead in excuse an uncle's partiality.   C.H.E.

Eton
October, 1882.

Introduction

"DEAR MOTHER,

I thought I had written you the last letter from England, but I was mistaken. I have not dared to read your letter all through; I will read it when I am safely in the steamer. I write to tell you something which I am sure you will like to hear. I went to see poor dear Aunt May's grave.... I am glad I went, it will do me good. Uncle Charlie and Aunt Mabel have offered father a return ticket in two years. I hope you will go to Eton for a thorough rest, after such hard work, and hope that I, on the contrary, after so much rest, am going to really hard work.

Good-bye, my loving mother.

From your very affectionate son."

Such were the last words written in England from a boy leaving a happy home to seek a livelihood in the far West. He was then eighteen years old, and the plan that had been roughly sketched out for him before leaving was, that he should go straight to the Agricultural College, Guelph, and stay there about a year, then proceed to Manitoba, hiring himself out to a farmer, with a view to taking a Government grant of land, and with the understanding that when he had proved himself worthy of the trust, money would be sent out, enabling him to start in whatever way he thought best. On the voyage he had the good fortune to make friends, whose kindness then, and throughout his sojourn in Ontario, went far to make him forget the painfulness of separation from home ties, and the strangeness of the new life. Their house was always open to him, and the sense of their exceeding kindness will always be treasured up by himself, as well as by his parents, with the sincerest gratitude.

Hillington Rectory
August 20, 1882.

$\mathcal{L}$etters

from a young emigrant

To his Mother

386, King Street, W. Toronto, October 7, 1880. 11.30 p.m. Written while waiting for admittance to the College. — *You see I am still here, and am in a very nice boarding-house, with some nice quiet fellows, much older than I am. Twenty dollars a month. Two are in government offices, two in banks, and three in various agencies in town. A lady named Fitzgerald keeps the place. I was presented at Government House to-day. They are very nice people. I am going over to Guelph*

to-morrow, to see the place. Mr. Jones very kindly introduced me to the head of the dominion bank here, the best
bank, in case he might be of any use to me in future. Very
kind of him. Of course it is very slow for me here, because
all the fellows are in office from 9.30 till 4. I go to Guelph
for good, when the new buildings are done, viz., November
8th. The weather here is lovely, though cold at night.
Mr. Smith has lent me a horse to ride whenever I like.
He is brother-in-law to Frank Jones, the fellow in the
house with me, cousin to the Mr. Jones with whom I was
staying. He, Mr. Smith, has a large farm about one
hundred miles from here, where young English fellows
learn farming. His advice is, steer clear of farming,
unless you want to do one of two things: if you have a
large fortune, and want to waste it; or if you haven't,
and want to live on dry bread and water all your life.
"Why don't you go into the bank at once, instead of
doing like every other young English fellow has done the
last years since I have lived in Toronto — go and learn
farming, get into slovenly habits, drink, and then get
tired of it, come back, be helped by some unfortunate
man, then disgrace him by being turned out for habits
acquired whilst thrown amongst low Canadian farmers
— low mean selfish men, who never spend a farthing
on anything but drink?" That was Mr. Smith's advice, who
came out as I have come out, took a farm, and ended by
going into the Post Office and getting to the top of the
tree with £3,000 a year now. He has very kindly asked me

46

to go with him up to his farm next week, "just to see your brother Englishmen, whom I make work like slaves, and nothwithstanding all my cautions. Well, you will see soon enough what whisky does for a man, having nothing but his own society to depend upon." Everybody certainly says the same thing, it is being dinned into my ears from morning till night. It really seems as if there were a conspiracy to kill in the birth every flickering love one might have, to do what one is sent out to do. I meant to write to uncle, but I quite forgot the post went out to-morrow, till I got into bed, so I had to hop out and write, for I promised him I would. Is Everard at home? I hope, oh I do hope he will get through all right! How do Frank and Bob like their school? How is Peg? How is Geoff? I have not had a letter yet since I left, so of course I am behindhand in the news. I hope grandmamma is well. I wish I had had time to say good-bye to aunts K. K. and Emma. You will be glad to hear I have been down at 8.30, an hour before breakfast, every morning. Has father tried a tricycle? Bicycles would not be the least use here. I saw a cart stick in a rut in Queen Street to-day, and it took five horses to pull it out, so you may imagine what state the roads in the country must be in. Give my love to all. Autumn tints, varying from transparent bright yellow to blood-red, — magnificent! All the trees so!

To his Mother

335, King Street, Toronto, Friday, October 22, 1880. — *Last time I wrote, I said how delightfully warm* it was. It is now awfully cold and bleak; bitter wind. On Tuesday and Wednesday it was frightfully cold; yesterday, it was so hot that I had to take my coat off whilst I was sitting still, sailing on the lake; to-day is what I call a great-coat day, underclothing included. I went to an evening gathering on Wednesday night — a compound of musical party and carpet dancing, — a very popular entertainment here, I hear. There was a great crowd there, and as the rooms are not large there was also a squash. I have got the invoice of something in bond from the Custom House, Guelph; I suppose it is my ring. I go up to Guelph on Thursday day next. I have got plenty of introductions to people at Guelph if ever I should happen to want them, but I don't suppose I shall, since there is not much time for going out there. I went to a musical five-o'clock tea last night; the same people, but only a choice picking of them. I knew these people from having travelled 2,655 miles with them, viz. from Liverpool to Toronto. Harold starts to-night for England. If there are any mistakes in my letter you must overlook them, because a rich old nigger who lives next door will insist upon playing the same tune (and that consisting of about ten bars) over and over again, which nearly drives me mad. He plays for two hours every morning, and gets through this tune about once in two minutes, thereby playing it about forty times a morning, allowing for stoppages; so I have heard the above tune six hundred times, not counting Sundays, on which he plays Moody

48

and Sankey's hymns over and over again. I suppose Everard is at home now, halfway through his examination. It has just this minute begun to snow hard; it snowed a little on Tuesday. I have just got your long letter of October 22nd forwarded from Guelph. I am so sorry about your missing the car, and I am very sorry for poor father. He must have felt it so much, though I could not help smiling at the thing as a whole. I am so sorry to hear that poor S_____ is dead; Geoff told me so too. I have had two letters from Frank, one from Peg, Everard, and Geoff. How I am going to answer them all I don't know. Listen! At last I have got hold of a fellow who has been at the farming College a year, and to Manitoba for two years. He says that the farming in Manitoba is as different from the farming in Ontario as the farming in Manitoba is different from the farming in England. In fact, from what I can see, the farming in Guelph is about the same as in England. All the stock comes direct from England, and the implements are exactly the same, and it is hardly likely that in Manitoba there will be an assortment of implements for thrashing, winnowing, etc. So this is what I am about to propose. A gentleman has offered to get me a place under a farmer in Manitoba, where I work for board, and pay about £2 a month for apprenticeship. Well! I propose to stop a year at the College, and learn the outline of farming, and get hardy, and all that sort of thing, and then go west and learn Manitoban farming for a complete year, and then take a farm. That is this gentleman's advice. He calls it making the best of a bad job; but then I intend to farm, if only just to get enough to support myself with, so that does not matter. The students say one can't do the real course under three years; but what I intend to do is to get really hardy, and inured to the climate, and the getting up cheerfully and going to bed early, so then I can learn the real farming in Manitoba. He says to make a farm answer it wants three fellows who can really get on well together — one to attend to the stock, and two to the tilling of the land, etc., — having a nice farm of about five hundred acres. Mr. McCaul says, "If any of your brothers are coming out, you learn clearing, and all that sort of thing; then get one of your brothers to come out straight to you, and you can teach him clearing and make him help you to get your farm into order; and let the other get a practical knowledge of stock, and by the time he has learnt his share (which he can do as easily in England as in Canada), you will have the farm ready with sheds, etc., to receive him and his share of the business." That is how he managed with two of his friends, but they did not get on well together. At Guelph I shall have to pay for everything myself, since I made application in my own name, so I should like to have a little money, say £10, in the bank always. As I told you, I have to pay $50 on entrance, and $10 for breakage, casualties, etc., besides washing and board, which is $2½ a week, i.e. 12s. I hired a pretty little cutter for a *week for a nominal price, $2, and had some splendid sails on the lake. And I thought how Margaret would have enjoyed it. I was thinking what a splended party Margaret, Frank and I should have made sailing along between two strange countries. Rather a strange thing happened last night. I was walking down King Street with one of my friends, and we met another man to whom I was introduced. I suppose he did not catch the name, for soon, in the course of conversation, he said, "That young Englishman" (myself) "who has just come out told rather a good story the other night, which I was told," and he proceeded to narrate it. We looked very grave, and he told us the story, which was a very good one, and made us roar with laughter. After he had done, I told him I was the person in question, and had certainly never heard the story before. I was told, afterwards, he was very fond of inventing stories and putting them down to other people. It is alternately raining and snowing now. Give my love to all.*

To his Mother

Toronto, October 29, 1880. — *I will not write now, because I shall be at Guelph, in my rooms, in time for Monday's post. I shall always send the diary separate from the letters, so that you may show it to whoever is interested in my welfare. I am somewhat close run for cash; after this unexpected interlude, I have only enough to pay the $11 entrance fee. I will write on Sunday from*

Guelph. I am going to a dance to-night, and to a five-to-ten "musicale" at the Norths' to-morrow, and go up to Guelph by the mid-day.

DIARY

Saturday, 23rd. — *Breakfast* 8.30; smoke and conversation with the other fellows till ten; took a walk along the lake with Beatty till 11.30; played billiards with him till one. Lunch, and wrote a letter to Margaret, and meditated till 3.45. Went to meet Frank at Parliament Buildings, as he gets out from work at four. Then we both went to a very nice tea-fight at Government House; music and singing. I was introduced to people, and asked to a dance on the 29th, which I accepted. We went to the Queen's Hotel after dinner, and spent the evening quietly, but musically, with some ladies we were asked to meet, and some American friends. Smoke; bed.

Sunday, 24th. — *Breakfast*; smoke; went to St. George's church in the morning with Beatty. I went to dine at Trinity College. I found one of the Sardinian passengers also dining there. I stayed till four, then went back to 336. Took a walk with Frank; 5.45 tea. Went to St. George's with Frank, then we went to supper at Trinity College. Smoke; bed.

Monday, 25th. — *Breakfast*, smoke, walk, billiards, and lunch, went in their usual routine. Read geography till four; went to meet Frank, and walk till five. Dressed,

52

and walked up to Heward's; dined, and went to hear Josepphè perform on the piano, and Remearqè on the violin. After dinner, meditated on the difficulties of the fifty-two Canadian counties, and capitals, in Ontario alone.

Wednesday, 27th. — *Same as usual till lunch. In afternoon P.P.C. calls on friends, all of whom have been very kind to me. After that I went to a five-o'clock tea (musicale) at Government House, and had a very pleasant time, since I knew everybody in the room. I went to a fancy bazaar in the afternoon, and I had great fun selling things, in aid of some Roman Catholic church.*

Thursday, 28th. — *Usual routine in morning; paid farewell visit at Government House in the afternoon, and afterwards went to a small family party at Trinity College. On Wednesday night 12° of frost. Thursday 40°.*

Friday, 29th. — *I wrote some letters in the morning; made some farewell visits to friends in the afternoon; went to a very nice dance in the evening; packed up all night.*

Guelph Agricultural College, Saturday, October 30, 1880. — *Came up to Guelph by the 12.15 train. Was asked to play in a football match against Guelph town directly I got out of the train. Played half back. Beat the town by two goals. Being All Hallow's e'en, or rather taken as such (there being no lectures on Saturday night), we went round singing for apples. I got nearly a* bushel in a bag. Apples in Canada are very cheap, and very good.

Sunday, 31st. — *Breakfast 7.30; church at eleven. Dinner 1.30; wrote letters; went for a walk by myself, a little low-spirited. Tea 5.30; went to evening church at seven; bed 9.30.*

Monday, November 1st. — *Breakfast 6.30; snowing hard; examination. Eight, English grammar; 10.30, English composition; 12.30, dinner; two, geography and arithmetic; six, tea. Went down town after tea; bought blacking brushes; mug, with which to wash my teeth; overalls (red canvas), and overall boots. Ten, lights out.*

November 25th. — *Carrying potatoes from the cellars to the house cellars — nice work for strengthening the back and rounding the shoulders. Went to a dance in the evening.*

November 26th. — *Wood-hauling, i.e. chopping, cross-saw cutting, and splitting in the bush. We light a tremendous fire, and sometimes our pipes, and then set to work demolishing the trees round us. The tree is cut down, sawn, and split fit for fires, in a very small interval. It is a bit dangerous, on account of the chips flying about the place. I have found that an Englishman has to learn a great deal in economizing his strength, and at the same time put strength into the blow. The first rule is, never lift the axe behind your shoulders, and bring it down with a sharp, clear stroke, never quite straight.*

54

November 27th. — *Instruction class, i.e. harnessing the teams, cleaning harness, and such petty jobs, which must be learnt. We get no pay for this. Did nothing in the afternoon, being a half-holiday; stopped at home and meditated.*

Sunday, 28th. — *Church. Dinner; Sunday school (teaching). Tea; church. Ordinary routine.*

Monday, 29th. — *Lectures in the morning; field-work in the afternoon; cattle, grooming, cleaning, feeding, and littering.*

November 30th. — *Making a ditch along a new road, standing up to my knees in water, freezing. I said to myself, two or three times in the course of the afternoon, "Everything must have an end."*

December 1st. — *Had an extra hour on stock, in lecturing, eight to nine. Yard man in the afternoon, cleaning out stalls, spreading manure, and feeding stock.*

December 2nd. — *I had what is called the "Boss job," viz. farm clerk; sit by the fire, in the boiling-house, keeping account of tools taken out and brought in, if in proper repair.*

December 3rd. — *Lectures during the morning. In the afternoon feeding the steam chaff-cutter; a nasty job, on account of the thistles and suffocating dust.*

December 4th. — *Half-holiday in the morning; skated. In the afternoon I was assistant shepherd; which* consists of carrying the food about, etc., but seeing very little of the sheep themselves.

5th. — *An extraordinary thaw, all day till seven, when it froze severely, making everything slippery; it was almost impossible to stand up. I went to church in the morning and evening, and took a class in the Sunday school as usual.*

6th. — *Turnip pulping in morning. Lectures in afternoon this week. Paid $50 50 cents to College bursar as fees. Thrashing in the experimental farm, where all the specimens of grain are tasted, bottled, and labelled, to the members of the Agricultural Union. I am a member.*

7th. — *Farm engineer,* i.e. *filling the engine with water, as of course all the water has to be withdrawn in the night on account of the sharp frost, — it is cold work early in the morning; splitting wood for the engine, and making one's self generally useful.*

To his Mother

School for Agriculture, Guelph, November 6, 1880. — *There is an old Haileybury friend of mine here. Of all the curious things in the world! He arrived to-night. How we laughed when we met each other. He came to, and left Haileybury at the same time as I did. He is a second-year student, and lives at Montreal. I doubled every one else's marks in the examination, getting 357 out of a possible 400. I am sorry you took so much* notice of my first two letters. You must remember I was terribly down-hearted, and not well. Now, I like the College work. Every morning up at 5.30, and I have never found the least difficulty in getting up directly the bell rings, and I have always had plenty of time to make my bed, carry away the slops, etc., before going down to prayers. Is not it curious? Don't you remember how difficult I used to find it, getting out of bed at eight or nine? Now I don't even feel a bit inclined to stay in bed after the bell rings at 5.30, though it is dark. If you had seen me pitching turnips into the cellars for four hours the day before yesterday, in drenching rain, you would have been surprised. I like all the foremen and masters very much, though they are rough, of course. I have been glazing all the double windows to-day. Rather arm-achy work. Please try and find my "Wilson's Inorganic Chemistry" — I think it is in the play house — and send it. By-the-bye, Mills said he would prefer writing to you for the $50 if I was at all hard up, because he wanted me to buy various text-books for the lectures, and I had to buy red canvas suit, top overalls, etc., so I have put $37 in the savings bank. My dear mother, I have only drank two glasses of beer since I have been in Canada; we can only get to town on Saturday and Sunday, and of course there is not beer up here. We have had two very good football matches since I have been here. I play three-quarter for the College team, and I am one of those comprising the OAS football committee. I like some of the fellows here very much. *The grub is somewhat changeable, sometimes very good, and sometimes bad; hardly time to eat it; and I have a thundering appetite after five hours's fieldwork.*

Toronto, Sunday, November 7th. — *We got a telegram to say that Upper Canada College from Toronto could not play us, so, as one of our masters had very kindly offered to give me a pass to Toronto and back, I profited by the opportunity of no lectures on Saturday, and an invitation to stay Saturday and Sunday with Frank Jones, to go down to Toronto for a party. It was a delightful one, and I went to dine with some other people afterwards. I went to dinner and supper at Trinity College, so it was a nice break. I start for Guelph by the 6 a.m. train, to be in time for lectures.*

TO HIS MOTHER

Ontario Agricultural College, December 8, 1880. — *I wish you all a very merry Christmas. It is not of course the first time I have been away at Christmas, only I feel more entirely separated than before. I shall think of you all on Christmas eve. I dine with such a dear kind old lady;...she always sends kind messages to me through Frank's letters, asking after my family, etc. I am cramming now for Christmas examinations. I was so pleased to get all your letters. I got the cheque, and had to pay a great deal out, on farming-books, etc., such as "Youatt on Sheep," "On Cattle," "The Model Grazier," "Stonehenge and the Horse." We must have them for the lectures. Last*

Sunday there was a tremendous thaw; everything melted, and it was quite hot. I went to church in the evening; and it was horribly wet and sloppy. When I came out everything was frozen solid. I wish I had got that pea-jacket Harold advised at Silver's. I have got no coat to work in, as of course my Norfolk jacket is too good — I mean that old home-spun; but it is cool work. My whole outfit was a mistake; as regards material, too good. Two good suits, and two really strong suits of rough tweed, are what a man wants, for a two years' equipment in this country. That knitted waistcoat of Aunt Fanny's was a godsend; but of course only to be used on swagger occasions! The most useful thing in my outfit was that woollen waistcoat with sleeves. I wear very little clothing in the house, so as to feel the difference when I go out. My costume indoors is — breeches, gaiters, slippers, flannel shirt, home-spun coat. Waistcoat, tie, and collar are quite unnecessary, not to say unheard of articles, as of course we have not time to change after work. I forgot to tell you we have a literary society here. I had to debate the Friday before last on "Resolved that ambition is a virtue." I was on the negative side and lost it. Last Friday I proposed the following debate: "Resolved that Vanity is conducive to the happiness of man." The positives got the debate. Next Friday the debate is "Chewing is injurious to the health." The fellows chew here to the most disgraceful extent, they make the walls and floors simply "hoggish." Besides the debates, poetry and prose are read. We have a president,

59

vice-president, secretary, critic, a committee of five. Every member pays twenty-five cents, and is bound to perform once in every term. Last Friday, one of the old country fellows was censured and expelled the meeting, for repeated disorderly conduct; he came in again, and in the end had to be carried out.

To his Mother

336, King Street, Toronto, December 27, 1880. — *You see I am in Toronto for my holidays. I had intended stopping at the College, and I did stop till the ten train, on Christmas day; but I found it altogether too hot for me up there. What with shifting me from one room to the other, to scrub the floors, and making me be in at 9.30, I thought the sooner I sloped the better. I was sorry, because I should have learned a good deal in farming those two weeks. I spent a very pleasant Christmas evening at the Trinity College. We drank "Absent friends." After dinner we drove to the family conclave, at the house of the head of the family. It was very nice, and reminded me forcibly of all at home....I was very tired, as I had had very little sleep the last week and a half, over the horrible examination papers. Toronto is much warmer than Guelph. When I come down to Toronto, I sometimes go about in a Norfolk jacket, without waistcoat or greatcoat. I don't know why, but I cannot write a letter to-day. I don't feel quite so well as usual. I suppose it is being so far from home at Christmas. I see in the newspapers that the weather in England is beautiful in a warm point of view. Now, mother dear, I must say good-night, and write another letter when I feel in a better mood. I think the examinations must have knocked me up a little. I hope you all had as merry a Christmas as possible.*

To his Mother

Sunday, January 2, 1881. 336, King Street, Toronto. — *I see you have sent my letters to Trinity College. I am going to stay there next week. Whilst I am at Guelph College it is impossible to be self-supporting, for the simple reason the pay we get for working full hours (and I always do work full hours) does not cover board and washing, which comes to $2 80 cents per week. Remember that if the authorities get so much as an inkling that Bob is thinking of farming in Iowa, they will fire him out before he has been there a day, Iowa being in the United States. The other day the Agricultural lecturer asked one of the fellows to describe how he should proceed on taking up land? "Well! when I get down to Minnesota I shall first do so and so." Lecturer: "Well, the sooner you do it the better; you can go and pack up your trunks now, and a team shall be ready to take you to the station, for the eleven train." They lent him money to get home, and sent him away at once. I had to kiss the Bible, and swear an oath, and sign a document, I was going to remain four years in Canada after leaving the College, when I sent in my request for admission. It is the dearest wish of my heart to be self-supporting, and my Irish friend and I have* often spoken together about going to Manitoba in April. There are a great many things I have been obliged to buy — boots for dirty work, the overalls, moccasins, etc., and many books to enlighten my mind on farming, draining, hedging, etc. So, if you have no objection, I should like to begin my struggle in April. I do not call the College life at all disagreeable. Hard work I like: besides, one is not bound to work at the College; but I think if you were to ask the foreman, he would tell you I always work hard and appear to like it. Do you remember that day in the hay? I had a feeble sort of idea I was working then. The fellows often hear me begin to laugh in the middle of work; I tell them it is my own thoughts: it is really because I am thinking about that day, that feeble imagination. Thank you for the things you sent, I will write to grandmamma next week, and give her an account of my gaieties, which will be more amusing to her than my farm labours. I went to four dances last week, and am going to five this; I don't dance, so I engage the ladies to sit the dances out — a very common proceeding here. I am lucky, and my cards for next week's dances are full. It is very cold here, on account of the winds; and I have never repented having given $9 for a fur cap, since I should have had no ears by this time, if I had not had one. They have a curious custom here of calling on New Year's day: all the ladies stop at home, the table spread with delicacies of the season, and wine, tea, and coffee. Then all the gentlemen call, and say,

"Happy New Year. Weather cold. Good-bye." I know
some who have called on as many as 130 different
families, between 11 a.m. and 6 p.m., driving from one
house to another.

To his Father

January 26th, Guelph. — *I got your letter last night.
Thank you very much for it. I can't get a definite answer
yet, about Bob's admittance to the College. Though I
should like to see him very much, I think it would perhaps
be better to wait till October. He will be nearly seven-
teen. His three years' course will take him up to twenty.
The lectures are decidedly hard work to get up properly,
and if he is going in for stock-raising he must get up
all his lectures well, both in theory and practice. It is
only six months more or less, and if mother thinks he had
better begin at once, I am sure I can manage it, though
there are many applications. I have been given a return
pass to Chicago, 450 miles from Toronto. I think I shall
take advantage of it at Easter, since board on the train
is nearly as cheap as anywhere else, and very nice besides;
and when one gets an opportunity of going to one of
the most flourishing towns on the continent by merely
paying one's board, it ought not be missed; besides, I
want to try and find something for myself. Mother wants
me to be self-supporting, and of course that is impossible
here. Thank you for the things from Silver's, it was the
most acceptable birthday present I could wish for. The*

63

*duty is frightful here. I had to pay 24s. on £5 worth.
We drill indoors at present, which is a consolation. Please
tell my brothers that they all seem rather good at beginning letters, but decidedly bad at finishing them. I act
"Larkspur" at our entertainment on the 18th. I am on the
committee of five, selected by the school to carry out the
entertainment, and I am vice-president of the literary
society. All the Englishmen here are popular, which will
be a consolation to you as far as Bob is concerned.
Lectures at 9 a.m., so I must close. Love to all.*

To his Mother

Oac, Guelph, February 6th. — *I have just received
your letter telling me your intentions concerning Bob. I
have made strict inquiries from every sort of person concerning farming. Bob could no more leave the College
after three years' course, and farm a thousand acres,
than fly to the moon. They teach you to tend stock, and
to judge stock here, but they do not teach you to take
care of yourself. Bob would have to rough it as foreman
in some stock ranch for two years, to get used to all the
tricks of cattle-dealing; a man to run a thousand acres,
must be thoroughly used to cattle-dealing, and also
sharp, and well up in his work. I hope I have not exaggerated the hardships of the College, because you seem
to think I have borne everything so well, when there
really was very little to bear. Of course it is uncomfort-
able working in the College; but it is almost worth being*

out to be able to come into the warm house as ravenous as a wolf. I like the outdoor work immensely, but I do not care for the lectures. The rooms are tremendously heated with steam, a nasty sleepy heat, which always makes it hard for me to keep awake. It was 27° below zero last Thursday at eleven o'clock, whilst we were out working, and it was a case of continual motion to keep warm. It is raining hard now, and everything is frightful. It is called "January thaw," and is a little late. The snow does not finally go till the end of March. Bob can be admitted to the College. I was thinking of copying out my diary for January, but, looking over it, I see nothing but the same round of work you have already seen. How exciting the ice and snow must have been for my brothers and sisters! How they must have enjoyed it! That suit of pilot cloth has been of immense use to me. When I go out it saves me wearing a heavy ulster, as of course it is too good to work in. It is frightful the way one gets through clothes here. The heavy strains lifting things, tears one's coat behind; trousers catch on nails, and I don't know what else. . . . Love to all.

To his Mother

OAC, Guelph, March 2, 1881. — I enclose one of the letters from the gentleman to whom I propose to go. The work will be harder there, but I shall learn more, and Smith is a thorough English gentleman, which is a great deal in Canada. He is a thorough master of farming, practically, not theoretically, as a great many with other means are. I think I have already told you he has one of the best appointments here, and only goes up to the farm on Saturday night till Monday. His wife and children are there almost always. I shall learn a great deal of farming, but, still more, gain much in interest — a great thing in Canada — by meeting influential people. I jumped at his very kind offer, made, when he heard me saying it was a mistake taking so much time up at College on lectures. The weather changes horribly every day, sometimes raining hard, and warm, next day 50° above zero and a stinging wind, which knocks one up very quickly. I got a very nice letter from grandmamma; she seems very well in spite of the weather you seem to be having. I have nothing new to tell you; life goes along at a jog-trot. I am in the carpenter's shop, grinding, chopping, and planing beams, rafters, and logs, for the new implement shed. — With love to all, your very affectionate son.

OAC, Guelph, March 9, 1881. — As regards going to Smith and leaving the College, my object is this: If I go to Eastwood for six months, Mr. Smith will have an opportunity of judging what I am most suited for. He is a man of strong common sense, very strict, having un-bounded contempt for anybody who is at all lazy, and he has a habit of telling them so, in a very short time, but he is a very kind man underneath his outer coat of roughness, and you can judge by his very kind letter to me. He has visited the OAC, and does not like it for any man going in for general farming, though he considers it a good place for a man going in for stock-raising, since there are splendid thoroughbreds, and one is taught the good points, and how practically to judge cattle.

OAC, March 22nd. — *We are now in the midst of examinations preparatory to breaking up for Easter; I shall be glad when I am out of this, as I want to be doing something definite as soon as possible. I hope you got the report of the* OAC *for* 1880. *It is very cold at night here still, but actually hot in the day time, they say it is frightfully hot here in summer. Send me out some light homespun clothes. Of course for work in summer I shall wear my flannels and knickerbockers; but in town, and on Sunday, I must dress respectably in honour of my "guardian," I might almost call him. I don't know why, but the Canadians have a greater prejudice against knickerbockers, even than the French have. We have had four months and a half of sleighing now, and four days' thaw. Last Sunday the snow had disappeared with rain, but it snowed all Sunday night and Monday, and the ground was covered again. To-day it is beautiful: a clear bright blue sky, and sun that makes the air warm and nice. I am sure you envy me! I have kept my diary regularly; I find it comes in very usefully. The College expenses are $3 30 cents. We work four hours a day in winter, and get two cents an hour, on account of the scarcity of work. In summer, strong and experienced third-year students only get eight cents an hour; second-year* students, six cents; first year, four cents. That is, then, I, a first-year student, only get in summer harvesting four cents an hour, or ninety-six cents per week — except in July and August, when we work the full ten hours a day, there being no lectures. So that I am about $2 34 cents, or 9s. 6d., to the bad every week, as a rule; so that it is quite as expensive, while learning less than at a farm. The bursar told me, the bill for a first-year student from November to April would be about $42, which I must pay before I leave at the end of March. None of the fellows are allowed to stay in College during Easter and midsummer holidays, so I am afraid I must ask you for $9 to pay my three weeks' lodging at Toronto, before I can go to Eastwood, since Mr. Smith cannot have me till the first of May. Paying one's way at the OAC is impossible; I work hard and get the same as fellows who loaf about the place the whole time. The College is good for stock-raising, because they have the best breeds, and feed them as a model farm ought to do. A boy cannot live here, and during his holidays in some other place, under $125 for board and washing. When Bob comes out, I shall be able to take him to the College and introduce him to my friends, and I hope he will be as happy and comfortable with his companions as I have been. I have no debts, or anything to weigh on my mind, and I am looking forward to the time when Uncle Charlie fulfils his promise and sends you on a trip to Canada. The only skeleton in my little cupboard of life is, When shall we all be gathered round the Christmas board together again?

To his Mother

336, King Street, Toronto, May 1st. — *I expected to be up at Eastwood by now, and was waiting to tell you how I liked it, but I was prevailed on to stop a little longer to see some sports here. It would be wiser to pay Bob's college expenses from home, and allow him £2 a month to cover all other expenses. Canvas overalls can be bought good and cheap in Guelph. White linen trousers, ordinary cricket shirts, very useful for summer wear. Bob had better bring some cloth with him, both for himself and me; you can get things made cheaply here, but the cloth is dear. I am quite brown and sunburnt already. I get up at six, and row round Hemlar Island by myself, a distance of six miles; I find it keeps me in good health and spirits. This weather is very trying. Last Sunday it was 87° in the shade, and all last week it was hot, while to-day it is cold and chilly, with no sun at all. I must write and congratulate Frank and Bob on their success in the athletic games. I find some difficulty in writing, because I have got a large gathering on my right-hand wrist. I think it came from knocking my hand against a rusty nail in launching the boat. My arm is swollen, and I have had to go back to my old enemies, "poultices." Toronto is a splendid town, almost every house connected with a central office by telephones, so that one can order carriages, food, or anything in a very short time. The fire-brigade in Toronto consists of thirty-seven different halls, connected with fire-alarms within a hundred yards of every house in Toronto; and forty seconds after the fire-alarm is sounded, the hose and fire-escapes are at the burning house. There are two daily papers at Guelph, and five in Toronto, besides innumerable weekly ones. There are fourteen different churches in Guelph of various denominations, and very good clergymen.*

Here end the College and Toronto letters, and as the list of clothes sent for his brother's outfit may be some guide to others intending to emigrate, it is here given: —

6 shirts, white   8 collars
6 coloured   6 collars
6 flannel   3 night-shirts
9 pairs of cotton socks   6 pairs of wool
6 pairs of thick stockings
12 pocket handkerchiefs
3 suits of under clothing   2 thick jerseys
1 suit of dress clothes   1 best for Sunday
1 stout tweed for winter
1 suit of homespun for summer
1 pilot jacket   1 thick pair of cloth trousers
1 suit of corduroys
1 pair of breeches and gaiters
old clothes to work in
2 pairs of buck-skin gloves
2 strong pairs of top boots — everyone works in them
2 ordinary pairs of boots, but without nails — they rot the
    leather
1 pair of slippers   1 billycock hat
1 cloth cap with fur over the ears
1 knitted waistcoat with sleeves
2 pairs of knitted gloves without fingers

To his Mother

Eastwood, Ontario, May 18, 1881. — *I am now at Eastwood and have been here for a fortnight, and have very little time to myself. I get up when I like, which is generally 6.15; clean harness, carriage, horses; plough, sow, feed; ordinary farm work. Such a life! Best in the world. Most beautiful place I ever was in. Trees, and park magnificent on a small scale. A fellow named Jones is with me, a nice fellow and devoted to farming, and making money. Just the fellow for me. He of course knows more about farming than I do, and I hold my tongue and learn as much as I can. Now listen: I have, as the Canadians say, "struck out" i.e. found the animal I wanted, — a man who has really spent three years in the Saskatchewan valley; and what's more, I am going up there next March with him, and we are going to rough it. The man told me the place is so rough at present, that it would be impossible to take a woman up there: I don't mean I am thinking of marrying — far from it; I am only giving you an idea of the place. Beautiful farming country, 160 acres for grant, $2 50 cents after that, only $1 paid down, and if you clear fifteen acres a year they give you back your mortgage on the other $1 50 cents. Now, I am not joking; I have been cooled down by hard work. He and I start together, half bush, half prairies. We can take up our grants, and with our intro-duction to the surveyor, I hope we shall be able to pick out our land, or, what is better, get reliable advice from* *the surveyor. If you take my advice you will send Frank out next March, and I will take him with me — labour up there is $2 50 cents (10s.) a day, so a hand extra is worth a good deal, — as you know Frank and I have always had a more than brotherly affection for each other and I should like him to be with me. My companion understands lumber, and I am a good hand with an axe. I am gathering information from reliable quarters, so as to be able to tell you more about it. I now drink nothing but the mildest beer. Whisky is the curse of the country, and a law has been made in certain counties, that nothing under ten gallons shall be sold. I have never tasted it. Once taste it, and they say it is like opium — it is nearly impossible to give it up. It is a curse to a Canadian but a double curse to an Englishman. The climate won't stand it, the rapid changes in the climate weaken the constitution. Yesterday I had on white flannel shirt, linen trousers, and a straw hat with a brim a foot broad, and I was dripping with perspiration. To-day I worked very hard, flannel shirt, cloth waistcoat, breeches and gaiters, and felt hat, and I was cold. Yesterday sun, to-day no sun. But now about work: I could have got my board for my work and $10 to boot, twenty times over if I had liked, but I wished to look round and take notice of every bit of farming I can pick up. If you are your own master, and are in a hurry to start, you can learn more by taking a plough, and doing a little broad-cast just as you like. I don't spend a cent out in the country except the $16 a* month for board and washing, and the travelling expenses when it is necessary, to see cattle with Smith, and buy and sell, and see how bargains are worked, which is good practice. My friend and I are going to take a log hut with us for the winter, and we are going to do everything ourselves, cooking and all. The Smiths go to England, and there will be nobody up here. We shall do as much lumber-hauling and sawing as possible, and keep our eyes open: so I hope this $16 a month won't go on after October. At present I am a little short of cash, from my confounded extravagance in town. I had to stop a month in Toronto before I came, and that was $22 for board at once. That is why I am in such a hurry to get to the north-west, to show you that I can do something besides continually writing for money. It makes me mad to think of it: £4 a month till October, and then £2 till April, and then I hope I shall be safely launching myself into the stream of money-making. I keep a close diary now of every cent I spend, what I do, and what letters I write; and the contents of my letters in an abbreviated form, in another book. If anybody happens to ask what would be a suitable present for me to start with to the north-west, a breech-loading gun, or a box of tools for heavy carpentering, would come in remarkably handy. It is now 2.30, and I have to be up at six, pick the stones off three fields, mark those which are too big with stakes, to prevent the reapers being broken in harvest, and I don't know how much more work. So good-night.

To his Mother

Eastwood, May 31, 1881. — *I have written to ask a man whether he can find me any employment at Portage. If he can, I shall go up there; but I shall want money — it will cost me by emigrant train £6. He would probably give me my board, and about $12 a month to start with. It is a six days' journey by express from here. If he can't take me, I shall hire myself out to some farmer (labour is scarce), and I shall get about $10 a month and board I hope, but there is a great prejudice against English gentlemen — they are generally lazy and proud, and do little work. I am at present without a cent; I have just spent my last for a stamp for this letter, and by the time I get an answer to this I shall owe two month's board. I think now it was a mistake coming here, as I am afraid I must offend Mr. Smith by having come at all if I leave so soon. As for writing articles for a newspaper, after a hard day's work it is almost impossible to concentrate enough energy (especially of the brain) to write essays; and you know, dear mother, I have not enough stuff in me to write articles for papers or periodicals. From continued intercourse with the working class, I find it hard enough to speak the Queen's English. I will let you know directly I get an answer from Portage. The mosquitoes make life a torture here at times; they have bitten me till I am twice my ordinary size, on face, arms, and neck; but they go away in the middle of June, I am told, and I certainly fervently hope they do. You* must excuse the dulness of my letter, but I have had a hard day's work and am very tired. We have at present over 150 head of cattle on the farm, and I have to draw water out of the wells, in the different fields, and fill the troughs morning, noon, and night. We ship thirty-nine head of the finest three-part bred cows you ever saw to Winnipeg on Thursday and I shall be glad when they are gone — it will be a load off my mind, because I have to remember every beast, so as to know which are to fill the contract and which stop. We are having a terrible drought, 88° to 98° in the shade, and no rain for three weeks; almost unheard of, as this is the season we depend on for rain. Grass drying up, instead of growing for hay. Fall wheat pretty good, but grain sown since winter utterly dried up, not sprouting at all. Love to all.

To his Father

Woodstock, July 7, 1881. — *Came here July 4. In defiance of telegram and letter I am now on a farm. I have left Eastwood for two months, since I think I shall be able to get a better idea of farming, in the most important season of the year, by being in a regular farm. In a monetary point of view there is not much difference, but still some, and every little helps. Hours: get up at 4.45. Grind mower-knives, fetch in water, light fire, etc. Breakfast at six; 6.30 to twelve, ordinary routine of field-work, viz., toss and cock hay, hoe potatoes and turnips, or cut thistles, dinner 12; one to six ditto, draw in hay, 6.30 tea. If there is anything to be done after tea, such as cock hay, we do it. Bed nine sharp. It is a 270-acre farm, and two other boys and myself get in, and put all the hay in the lofts. The boss has got the reputation of being the best farmer, and raising the best crops, and treating his men best for thirty miles round. He is a good-natured old Scotchman of the labourer type. He just mows the hay with the machine, and horse-rakes with the sulky rake, as he is getting old. He has undertaken to put more solid farming into me in two months than I should learn at Eastwood in two years. Mr. Smith said I should never be able to stand the life, and upon my honour I winced when I saw where I should have to sleep, in the same room as the two farm boys. The boss is not married, but keeps a housekeeper. This is an experiment to me whether I can really stand hard work, and I must own it is harder than I bargained for. Getting in the hay, hitching, and getting it into the lofts, is a tremendous strain, since I have to keep up with the other two, who are three years older than I am, and used to it all their lives. The farm is three-quarters of a mile from Woodstock, and five and a half from Eastwood, so when we do not work too late, I shall take the train to Eastwood, and sleep there Saturday night. My friend will drive me back on Sunday night, so I shall not get too rustic. I am sure you will excuse my going against your orders. But if I can stand two months without running I shall know myself, and be able to rely on my* determination, and the power to back it up. Thank you very much for the £10. It came just in time to pay off all arrears, and I have something over for the next two months. You may always think of me as being happy. My letters may be downhearted sometimes, and that is partly the reason I did not write last week. I was in the dumps, and I was afraid my letter might make you think I was unhappy. I am quite happy in this little house, with plain labourers, and bacon and potatoes for every meal; and of course I am learning far more here, because I have to do my share or leave. Old Andrew says it is no use trying to learn farming if you only do the easy jobs. He is a kind old man, and teaches me to the best of his powers, and that is saying a good deal, because of course he has to leave off his own work to show me. I will write and tell you more early next week, but it is 9.30, and I must be up at 4.45 to-morrow. Don't be uneasy about me dear mother; if I find the work too hard, I shall go back to Eastwood, since Mr. Smith says he shall be glad to see me whenever I choose to come. He only has friends up on Sunday, so I shall see all the rank and wealth anyhow. Love to all.

To his Mother

Woodstock, July 12, 1881. — I am learning farming practically now, there can be no mistake about that. I cannot exactly explain my reasons for leaving Eastwood for the two months. I think it arose more from feeling *that I was wasting time and not doing as much as I ought to be doing. You tell me to let you know my ups and downs, and never hide anything from you: I certainly never shall. I keep my diary for my own use, and reference, but I am going to send it to you at the end of the year, knowing you will make a full allowance for any little things you may not exactly like. I want to say a good deal, but I can't put it into words; but one thing I must say, and that is — tell Frank from me, to strain every nerve, to work for what he is trying for; that if emigration is the alternative, it is better to live in England with almost nothing than farm in Canada and be rich (if rich he ever can be). Tell him from me, to give up every amusement till he has reached the goal he wishes to arrive at. Ask him which is best off — he, lying under a shady tree, reading his book quietly, with something definite to look forward to, and almost certain, if he chooses to strain every nerve for it, — he, who will always then be living among civilized people, with somebody pleasant to talk to, and his parents within a day's journey, — or myself, getting up at 4.45, working hard all day in the broiling sun, the perspiration streaming through my clothes, and towards evening tired to death; and latterly having to turn out and get up hay till 9.30, with nothing to eat but a little bit of bacon and potatoes, and bread and butter: an indefinite future, among a few emigrant labourers, far away from home, with irregular means of communication, having to drudge through the*

78

heat of summer and the cold of winter? Last Sunday, for example, 98° in the shade, working in the broiling sun, pitching hay in a great hurry for fear of rain. In the loft where we were packing the hay, there were myself and another fellow, and it was so terribly hot and stuffy there, that the fellow fainted, and the whole of the work fell on me. When I came out of the loft, every time in the broiling sun, it seemed positively cool comparatively. Of course that was an exceptional day, and haying is the worst and hardest work in the year. That day we worked till ten, and packed the hay by lantern light. I walked upstairs, lay down on my bed, and slept till morning just as I was, I was so tired out. I am staying to find out how much determination I have, so as to find out in time whether I am morally and physically strong enough for the work I have chosen myself. By the time this reaches home, holidays will have begun. It will be the time I shall miss home most, but I shall know I have done more in the game of life since last August than all the other years put together. I must write to grandmamma the first opportunity, but I have not much time now; we often work till nine, then I tumble into bed as quickly as possible. *

*When he could get away, he was always made welcome to a substantial supper by a kind friend, from whose house his letters were always written, his parents most gratefully acknowledge this thoughtful kindness.

To his Mother

The Farm, July 26, 1881. — *I have just read your and father's letter. Firstly, business. One pair of fisherman's boots, and one pair of thick common boots will do splendidly. Moccasins are useless in a farm, on account of the manure and stuff which soaks through. I used them last winter when working in the bush. Both Mr. and Mrs. Smith kindly wish me to come back when I have worked my time out, and I probably shall. I go out there every Sunday, and I slept there Saturday night. I am afraid my last letter was not a very reassuring one, but I was rather downhearted. I hope you saw that, and knew it was only a passing fit. Now I shall describe to you a Canadian harvest. Our farm is 270 acres, mostly laid out in grain. The men are as follows: — The boss, Jem, hired from May to October. Sam ditto. Ted (self), July and August. All living in the house. Pattison, a Lincolnshire man, from near Wisbeach, hired by the day. Niel, hired by the day. Boss drives the reaper; Jem, Sam, Pattison, Niel are the binders; Ted, shocker. We start, say a twenty-acre field of fall wheat, as follows: Directly after breakfast, 6 a.m., Jem starts for the field; mows it all round, with Sam beginning the other side; Niel and Pattinson, following, are binding. I, meantime, am harnessing the boss's team, and getting two pailfuls of water with oatmeal in it. When all this is done, we wait till the reaper has taken four turns, then each binder has a row, then we*

80

all start; the machine making four rounds to the four binders one. I, myself, always close behind, shocking them up directly they are thrown from the binders' hands. Last week we cut thirty-six acres of fall wheat, bound and shocked it; and six of barley. One day and a half was wet. We have now fourteen more of fall wheat, and eight of barley, to cut. Then we draw it all into the barns, and thrash it out; and start on the oats, peas, and spring wheat. No stacks here, because the grain grows in the stack directly. I enclose a bit of the Toronto Globe, about the north-west territory. Of course it is greatly exaggerated; but there is probably some foundation for what it says. If all goes well, I shall launch out my little craft next March. I shall get my grant, and then see which is best — to hire out for the summer, and draw wood in winter for building directly spring comes on, or what. I should like to work through the summer near my own lot, building my hut in the odd hours, and at the same time making friends with my employer, so that he will take an interest in me, and give me a hand and good advice. When I am settled, I shall get you to find me some intending emigrants, as labour up here is scarce in harvest and seeding time. I am beginning to have some confidence in myself. My plans don't assume such large proportions; my ideas are connecting themselves; and, in short, I am beginning to feel that when I say I will do it, the thing must be done, through thick and through thin. I am my own tutor, but my purse, this time five years, will be my examiner, and dollars and cents will represent the marks I have made in the preliminary. I think Bob will like the College — well fed, well roomed, and always warm. Tell me as soon as you can what steamer he intends starting by. I wish you could see my head; I had every morsel of hair clipped with a machine to the sixth of an inch, to keep my head clean in harvest. Looking-glasses are an unknown luxury in a farm, and there is just a tin bowl of out doors to wash in. Every second day I get into the wash-tub in the barn. There are three things which, above all others, the hired man cannot understand — night-gown, tooth-brush, and prayers. The Canadian Jack is as good as his master, and it is rather a takedown to family pride to see, at every word, that the men don't see I was ever a bit better than they see me now (in fact, I don't know whether I ever was). "I tell ye what; some o' the fellows up town (shopkeepers) is pretty stylish; they'd never even look at the likes of you and me, Ted." Love to all.

The Farm, August 14th. — I am sorry to say I have been rather irregular with my letters lately; my excuse is work. I have just finished my first thrashing. I was carrying grain with another man — about the hardest work of the lot, since the grain comes out quick enough to keep two sacks continually going. I am really now beginning to take a decided interest in farming, as there is at least one feature in it which you know I like — change, a great variety of things to do and attend to. I am keeping my *diary very carefully. I am told since I have been here on the farm, notwithstanding the diet and early hours, I am looking much better than I have since I have been in Canada. In fact, I may say that these two months of simple labouring life, like a plough-boy in England, will have been amongst the happiest and most undisturbed in my nineteen and a half years' residence in the world. By-the-bye, I must tell you of a peculiar thing which takes place. When I have been out at work, and come in to meals, my face and arms are covered with salt; in other words, my perspiration is so impregnated with the salt of the meat, etc., that I eat, that, when it evaporates, the salt is left, and it presents a most peculiar appearance. The thermometer, two days running, was 102° in the shade, with a strong wind blowing which seemed as if it had come from a furnace. It is what the Canadians call a "wet-shirt day." Love to all.*

Here ends the two months' self-imposed probation with the kindly old Scotch farmer — a rough trial, almost too much for his strength, but one leaving behind it valuable experiences. He now returned to Eastwood, received and helped to settle his younger brother at College, and then started for the far West. The letters will tell under what circumstances.

To his Mother

Eastwood, October 6th. — *I have been intending to write for some time but have put off writing each*

83

day, waiting for further particulars. A little time ago, I got an offer of board for work in Beaconsfield, Manitoba. I have just accepted the offer willingly, for the following reason. I shall have the whole winter to judge what a new country is really like. I am sorry to leave Bob, who is in moderate spirits, but doing his best to get me to stop till spring. Of course it will be rather rough work out there. Only the other fellow and myself in the house, so we shall take turns by weeks, in cooking, housekeeping, etc. But I am impatient to start. One thousand five hundred miles on my journey will be a good start for the north-west. I hope I shall have enough money for the journey. Bob and I go to Guelph to-morrow. He is the most amusing fellow I ever met. . . . My movements are as follows: Guelph, Friday to Monday; Eastwood, Monday to Thursday; Toronto, Thursday to Monday; journey to Manitoba, Monday 17th till Thursday 20th. I have taken on myself the responsibility of going without your and father's sanction, hoping that you will not be annoyed on account of the short notice which I must necessarily give you, only knowing it myself in the last few days. "There is a tide in the affairs of men, which, if taken at its rise, leads on to fortune." I don't know exactly if it is a safe maxim to trade on, but in this case it seems to be a good one. Bob has already planned out his future career, but, like myself, he has forgotten that there are two or three impediments of an objectionable nature in his way. He seems to have made friends with several

84

nice people in the steamer — an easy task with him, since he is so light-hearted and gay; so I have no fears, as regards leaving him alone in Canada, though I am very sorry. He is the only person who has made me laugh, continually and heartily, since I have been in Canada, and his anecdotes made me die with laughter. I could not help crying a little when he described the Christmas dinner, and father proposing to my health. I think I was just then in the team travelling from Guelph to Toronto. When shall we all be assembled over the Christmas dinner again I wonder! and what a noisy lot we shall be — from austere pedagogue to noisy backwoodsman, from the old grey-haired father to the rising young engineer! A happy day to look forward to. I must go and pack Bob's things. I have not seen anything but his hat, which is squashed considerably out of its former shape. Love to all.

To his Father

Eastwood, October 19, 1881. — *I telegraphed for money because the place I am going to is sixty-two miles from any railway, or registered letter office, and I shall be there till April at least. I have been seedy and out of sorts for the last month, and can't shake it off.**

---

*Malaria fever had caused three deaths in the village, and all at Eastwood had been ill or unwell. He had escaped with sore throat only, and pain in his chest.

I don't know why, everything seems to be going wrong with me. I broke my watch glass twice, and a pipe I have had for three years, the same day. I could not go by the special to Manitoba to-day, for two good reasons — scarcity of cash, and my box, which Bob brought out, has not turned up; yet, after much telegraphing, it has been found, and I hope will soon be here. Bob seems to like College very much... both in mind and abode. I have felt too unsettled to write lately; indeed, at times, it was impossible, and sometimes if I had written, you would have thought either I was mad or on the verge of the grave. I feel being away from home more now, as have been used to being away for a year, but never more, and I think Bob's arrival has sent me into the dumps. I was very glad to see him, but he reminded me forcibly of home.... I determined to brighten up somehow, so I went the round of the exhibitions — the county exhibition at Toronto, the provincial exhibition at Hamilton, and the local exhibition at London. I saw many new Yankee inventions to economize manual labour. Now a man can cut hay, turn hay, load hay, unload it into the mow without touching it himself! Labour is scarce in some parts of the States, and necessitates these inventions. I wish I could invent something and make a fortune! With sincere love to all.

To his Mother

Eastwood, October 25, 1881. — *I hope by the time you get this letter, you will be having a good rest after your fatigues.*

November 7th. — I broke off to fetch something for Mrs. Smith, and did not resume quite so quickly as I meant to. Since I started this letter I have been in Guelph to get box and see Bob. I am now at Trinity College, on the eve of departure for Emerson. I go by rail to Emerson, sixty-five miles by stage afterwards. It is late in the year for business of this kind. I have been worried out of my life, for the last two weeks, by one thing and another, but have enjoyed my stay at Trinity College immensely, which, as you know, I always regard as my "Canadian home." I leave Toronto Tuesday. November 8th, 15.50 p.m. Arrive at Chicago, Wednesday, 9th, 7 a.m. leave Chicago, 10.5 a.m. Arrive at St. Paul's, Thursday, 10th, 5.50 a.m., leaving St. Paul's, 10th, 7.30 p.m. Arrive at St. Vincent, Friday 11th, 4.40 p.m.; Emerson, Friday, 4th, 10 p.m. I shall have to have my luggage examined twice. I left all my decent clothes and shirts at Eastwood, feeling they will be wasted up there. The kindness and forethought in packing by box was perfection itself, though I did not want the shirts just now. Please thank Aunt Fanny for the revolver, which is very nice, and the little ones for the pen, of which, by-the-bye, I have only found the paper that enclosed it. Will for the deed! I will write directly I am settled in my new quarters.

To his Mother

Cyprus Lodge, Manitoba, November 23, 1881. Received, December 15th. — *Here I am. I am sure you are anxious to hear how I like the life.*

First, Cyprus Lodge.

It is made of poplar logs with the crevices stopped up with mud. Inmates, Mr. Boulton and his sister. Half the inside is curtained off for bed-room. It has a floor (which is a curiosity in this part of the country) and a sort of ceiling composed of loose planks. Now I have a lot to say, and very little time to say it in. Two mails a week, Wednesdays and Saturdays. Boulton is a very nice fellow. His sister — his housekeeper. Boulton is at present in Emerson, 109 miles from here, fetching his mother, who has just come from down below, i.e. Ontario. As to my journey, I left Toronto 12.15 p.m. on Tuesday. On Tuesday afternoon we stuck on a grade, our train being very heavy, and had to wait, get up steam, back down and make a rush, which of course was fun. We crossed the St. Clair River at seven in the evening. The train being taken across in a steam-ferry. After this our luggage was looked over, as we were now in the States. My trunks were not opened, however, when I showed my checks for Emerson. The cars here were both crowded and close. At Lafeen, on the Chicago and GPR we had to wait from 1.15 to 6.15, as a freight train jumped the track, just ahead of us. It was a cold night, but we made a good fire in the waiting-room, by tearing up some of the platform, and so were tolerably comfortable. This was all new country, rough, and hardly worth settling. We got to Chicago at eight in the evening, instead of eight in the morning, but I managed to catch my con-

nection from Chicago to St. Paul's. We passed some of the most beautiful scenery imaginable. Chicago is an enormous town, you know, — 600,000 inhabitants. St. Paul's is a rising place, with mud up to your knees in the main streets, with about ten thousand inhabitants. The prairies are on fire in a good many places. I got to Emerson at five on Friday evening. Emerson has about nine hundred inhabitants. A slow, quiet place. I had to spend Saturday and Sunday in Emerson waiting for the stage, which started on Monday morning. Saturday and Sunday were nice warm days. I got up on Monday with a joyful heart to finish my tiresome journey, and the agony began. First, a strong head wind 15°. Before I got to West Lynne, three miles distant, my nose, right ear, three fingers were frozen. With the help of another man, I rubbed the frost out with snow, and went into a store and bound my comforter round my whole face. I had my fur cap over my ears.

Emerson to Mountain City, fifty-five miles in twelve hours. We started from Emerson at seven in the morning, slept at a farm-house, and got to Mountain City at seven next day; and I did suffer again — the wind seemed to penetrate to my very bones, through great coat, peajacket and all. People all wear buffalo coats here, and moccasins. I have at present three pairs of thick socks on, and moccasins, which I have been given by a fellow here very kindly, and very fortunately, as my funds are run out.

89

Mail between Mountain City and Darlington Hotel, fifteen miles in three hours. Mountain City has about one house in it, a store, and a saw-mill. I forgot to say about twenty miles from Emerson we passed through about fifteen Mennonite* villages, and saw plenty of Mennonites, dirty people. Darlington Hotel is a house by itself, which contracts for the stage-cart, and north of Mountain City.

Mail between Darlington Hotel and Beaconsfield, forty miles in twelve hours. This last part of our drive was on wheels, with about one foot of snow, and numerous drifts. I got to Beaconsfield Post Office, which is a shanty smaller than our own, at three on Wednesday, having suffered in the last three days more than I ever suffered in any three years of my life before. I had boots and one pair of socks, whilst moccasins and three pairs of socks, walking, is only just enough. The highest I have seen the thermometer since I have been here, is 12° below freezing point in the sun. When I got up this morning to light the fire, it was 38° below zero. "He who tastes Red River water always returns." I can believe it. I enjoy the weather — well wrapped up, plenty of work to keep me warm, wood to chop, cattle to feed, etc. I have had a great deal of conversation with Boulton. I propose taking up a section, 640 acres, which will

*A religious sect, so called from its founder Simonis Menno, a Frieslander of the 16th century.

cost me, the first year, 160 acres, nothing: second, 160 acres, $10; third, 320 acres, $54. Boulton says £400 will start me fairly. I am learning to bake and cook now. It is impossible to raise anything but potatoes first year; but it is imperative to do as much breaking soil as possible, so as to be ready to plough next season. So if you can let me have some money, I shall take up land early next spring, when I can see the land. it is a good and safe investment for any money, since land is going up at a tremendous pace. Sections are sold at $2 an acre, with twelve years to pay it in, at six per cent., so if you would like any more bought for Bob, it is as safe as the Bank of England. And a railway is being built through Manitoba now, in five different places, and emigrants are crowding in by every train. The mail goes soon, and I have three miles to walk for the post-office. They are all English round here. I sleep on the floor with blankets and buffalo robe — too cold for sheets. With love to all. . . .

To his Mother

Cyprus Lodge, November 30, 1881. — *Your letter is full of practical advice. I can milk, I can make butter, I can bake a little, etc.; in fact, I think I could bach it (i.e. keep bachelor's quarters) very comfortably, and with economy. Now to business. There is a lot (640 acres) close to here, the best land in Manitoba in a civilized spot, for sale, homestead, and pre-emption, 160 acres for nothing, 160 for $1 an acre, twelve years to pay it* in; 320 acres, $2 an acre, twelve years to pay it in. The land is valuable for this reason — a railway will run through it in two years. Fellows are now selling their lots for $4,000, with about $300 worth of improvements on them. So it is a safe investment for money, at ten per cent. (the least possible calculation). If you can give me money to start on, I could buy the land this winter. Thirty pounds would do that, but then there are my logs for my house, stables, etc., this winter, before March, that I may build in the autumn; breaking about twenty acres this spring with oxen. One can put nothing but potatoes in, first breaking, which would give me time to break a nicer lot for next year. I have talked all this over with Boulton, who has been four years in the country, and was the first to settle in the district. I am now qualified to look after myself; and as for starting, it takes three years to make anything but cover expenses, so the sooner started the better. This year I should break as much as possible, put in one acre and a half of potatoes, build my house, and save hay for my oxen, and a cow, probably, and have two pigs. Digging a cellar to keep the potatoes, and a well for water, takes time. Poplar logs to be sawn up for lumber, for my house, probably sixteen feet by twenty; and teaming to Emerson for stores, tools, window sashes, etc.; so, you see, a good start in the spring would be necessary. This lot is not open for settlement yet, so I should have to be ready with the cash to pounce upon it; and they are nice English people around here, who would be glad to help me and advise. Besides, it is unheard of! In the middle of one of the best districts, well settled, with a railway already surveyed, and a bonus of $70,000 promised, it will save taking things twenty miles to a market, and having to go 110 miles to Emerson to buy anything. Portage la Prairie is thirty miles north of this. The Boultons are very nice people, Plymouth Brethren, Bible reading, and prayer every morning and evening. Graham Boulton is a very sensible, nice fellow; it is he who advises me to stop my wandering, and settle here. He also showed me how he lost a year by having no one to advise him. So I really think, if I settle now, it will be better than waiting till I am twenty-four. Boulton has just come back from Emerson, with his mother, and I have been managing his farm in his absence. He has two lots, 1,280 acres, but only farms one. The other is for speculation. He expects to get $20 an acre for it in four years. I should like to begin at once, if possible; so I trust to your powers, dear mother, to give me help, both in money and advice. The country here is splendid, they say, in summer, so I have hopes that if I take up a lot, when I get my shanty fairly comfortable, you will brave the voyage, and come and spend one summer with me before long. At Eastwood I used to work in the kitchen-garden sometimes, so I know something of it. I should not buy a team of horses the first year, by which I should save one year's oats, which are 2s. a bushel here now; hay costs the trouble of

93

cutting and drawing in, and oxen thrive on it. I used to churn at Eastwood, and made the butter once or twice. Write and let me know your decision about the land as soon as possible. If you let me take up land at once, I should take up the whole lot, as I should not be able to get land adjoining, if I take less, when I wanted it. If I miss this lot, I shall start land-hunting directly the spring comes, and the snow clears. The land here is taken up at once, so the longer I wait the further west I shall have to go; in fact, this is the only lot for miles round, and this is vacant on account of a quarrel between the Syndicate and Government, as to whom it belongs. I will send my diary home as soon as the year closes. I shall anxiously await an answer. I can change Bank of England notes here, and registered letters are safe; and I shall perfectly understand the money is for land only. I meant to say a good deal more, but I have so little time. With love, etc.

To his Mother

Cyprus Lodge, Manitoba, December 4, 1881. — A merry Christmas to you all, and a happy new year. May the new year run in as happily with you as the old year is running out with me. There will be two absent ones from the flock this year at the Christmas dinner. I don't know where Bob will eat his, but I know where and what mine will be: roast beef (a great delicacy here) and prairie chickens, a bird with more flesh on it for its *size than any other I know, domestic or otherwise. I remember wondering last Christmas where I should be this; and now I look forward a year, and wonder whether I shall have a house of my own next year. Two railroads will pass within a mile of this next winter. The South-Western, and a branch of the* CPR. *If only I could get lot nine, it will be worth eight or ten thousand dollars this time three years, besides being the best farming district this side the water, and the healthiest. I think I told you the Boultons are Plymouth Brethren, and we have prayers morning and evening, and grace before and after meals.... I can't tell you now how much better I feel with this, than continually hearing religion ridiculed and made light of — it used to weigh me down so. These people quiet me, nothing worldly about them, not ever ready to pick holes and find fault; Graham Boulton lively and energetic, always ready to tell me about the land and* modus operandi, *to show me my mistakes, and take an interest in my learning. Mrs. Boulton is a mother to me. It is indeed a change. How long will it be, dearest mother, before you can come across the water to unseen lands, everything new about you, from the earth to the beautiful sky above you? Poplar, and a few oaks, are the only trees here, with balm of gilead, wild hops interlacing the scrub; roses, plums, gooseberries, strawberries, raspberries, cranberries, sprinkled in myriads around. He who has once pitched his tent by the Red River always returns. Well, I can well believe it, though.*

there are at present two feet of snow on the ground. For the last week the thermometer has ranged between 10° and 45°, for we have had a thaw, very unusual in this country, though it only lasted for an hour, and very nasty it is — wet through the whole time; it is much nicer and more comfortable at 10° below zero, than 25° above. It seems warmer, because the air is dry, and the snow crisp. This morning I was wandering about in search of the cattle, with those heavy top-boots, a foot and a half of snow everywhere, and three or four feet in many places. It is too damp at present for moccasins, the heat of the foot thawing the snow; thermometer about 22°. I run the farm at present, as Boulton is threshing about the place from six in the morning till seven in the evening. You should see the evening! full moon, clear sky, every star like an electric light. There are about twenty settlers in this township; "Waymanasi" is its name. Four years ago there was not a human being. Whisky is not allowed on account of the Indians. . . . Good-night.

To his Mother

Cyprus Lodge, December, 15, 1881. — As I know you are athirst for knowledge of the settlers's life, I will try and give you all the points worthy of discussion, so that you may be able to form both your plans and your advice for my future advantage. I. As regards money; II As regards time; III. As regards housekeeping.

I. Money. It is beyond the possibility of a doubt, that the first year the settler must have money enough to buy the necessities of life — oats for his horses, if he has any, (a wise settler will have oxen the first year, as it advisable to put nothing in but potatoes, as the ground never mellows properly with a crop the first year); also he has to buy tools, window frames, stove, cooking utensils, waggon sleigh, horserake for his hay, pigs, cow, lumber for the flooring of his house, etc. Shingles for his roof — they are like slates, only made of wood. Having told you, in a rough way, what he has to buy, I may now hint at the different methods settlers adopt of getting the necessaries. I know all the settlers around here, and they, without exception, have adopted one of three methods. 1. The older ones have some money of their own. The younger ones are given it by relations, who take an interest in their welfare. This is the easiest, and need I say it, as far as their farm goes, the best. 2. Are those who spend their summer up here, and have also some business down below (in Canada), either pig-smoking, or something of that sort. These are only the older people, who have a profession. 3. Are those who work in partnerships in twos. One goes and works on one of the railroads which are being made, in Manitoba, and the northwest, and makes money, which he sends to be laid out by his partner to their mutual advantage. This, I may add, is a method adopted by common labourers; no educated person could possibly stand the company of navvies, such as are employed in the far west, truly, the scum of the earth — Yankees, Irish, and Scotch, chiefly, who are used to spend their money, and any one else's they can get hold of, in drink, and other articles as useless. I have met one or two this summer, who tried the experiment, and gave it up as hopeless. It pays to get your land cleared by someone else the first year — cost $4 an acre, — since oxen are useless, as far as ploughing is concerned, to those not used to managing them. This I have direct and unanimously from the settlers about here. The settler will have plenty to do — geting ready for winter, building his house, etc. The greatest amount cleared in the settlement for the whole three years, is thirty-six acres; and to me, who am utterly untutored in rough carpentry, house and stables and cattle-shed will take an enormous time to put up. Log to draw out and hew; the latter, of course, I could not do, though cutting them down and drawing them out of the bush I could. Hew, is to chop into a square. So I should take three years at least before turning over a cent to my advantage, and the fencing my land in will take some time. I can cut the rails out in winter, but of course I cannot stick them up, on account of hardness of the ground. Suppose I do get twenty acres broken, there are only two months, May 15th to July 15th, for breaking, and back set it in the fall. I can raise twenty acres of grain the second year; say 15 acres of fall wheat, 2½ of oats, 2½ barley —

	Dollars	Cents
15 acres of wheat, at 20 bushels to the acre, = 300 bushels, at 75 cents per bushel	225	
2½ acres of oats, at 40 bushels to the acre, = 100 bushels, at 60 cents per bushel	60	
2½ acres of barley, at 30 bushels to the acre, = 75 bushels, at 65 cents per bushel	48	75
	$333	75

out of which I must feed my horse, buy my groceries and sundries, besides seed. I may have a calf, and some pigs; the latter I shall eat. I may have some potatoes to sell, but not many.

II. Time. There is little of this for a farmer to spare, on that which is not actual farming. In summer he is on the run all day. In winter the day lasts from eight till four; very short. He is employed in summer getting up his crop; breaking new land, and changing work with his fellow-settlers. There is very little hiring here; everybody changes work, i.e. settlers come and help you to do something — get in a field of grain, bind, shock, and draw it in; then you go and help these in their turn. In winter you are drawing out logs for new buildings, and for fencing new clearings, etc. I mention this, to show you it does not pay to raise butter, milk, etc.; you have not time. In summer you have to bake at night. The seasons are short here. It is light in summer from 3.30 till 9;

and with so few hands, it is impossible to do a variety of things.

III. Housekeeping. May be divided into three divisions: 1. Marry; 2. Sisters or young brother well versed in such things; 3. Bach it. I have to do with the third. The bachelor lives on pork and bannocks, as a rule; never sweeps his house out, or very seldom; generally hoes the floor once a month. It is the most expensive way, because he has no time to make bread often, or even butter, in summer, or puddings, or soups with vegetables, which saves the meat — and meat is expensive, pork being 11 cents per pound; and he also has to eat syrup instead of butter. I am now quoting incontestable truths; therefore my advice to the settler is, marry. *Every girl is pounced on directly she puts her face inside the settlement. Young fellows get so sick of the monotony of baching. I hope to get Frank out, after a year or two, to help me; or marry — some young lady well versed in scrubbing, washing, baking, dairying, getting up at 3.30 in summer, 5.50 in winter; strong nerves, strong constitution, obedient, and with money. Where can I find the paragon? Ever since I have been up here, I have been studying the whole thing; walking a mile and a half after tea, to have a talk with one settler and another, to get advice, and gain information, with the full intention of starting on my own hook, by hook or crook, in the coming spring. Now to come to the point. The universal advice is, if you have the money, buy some discontented man out, and start where* he left off, thus gaining three years. Now, here is the curious part of it: everybody round here declares he has the best farm in Manitoba; he would not part with it, or trade, for worlds; everyone seems as content as possible, with one exception. About a mile and a half from here, is the best, but it costs $1 an acre more to clear, either in hire or trouble, which makes $5. He has a house, 24 ft. by 20 ft., staircase, five windows, upstair room, etc., not finished yet, but when finished, which he agrees to do before spring, $450; stable, to hold two teams, $100 cow-stable, to hold cow and calves, $80: total, $790; besides fences, etc. He will get the deed and hand over with the property. He has been on the land for four years, and wants $2,500 — about £520. Now for the reasons I tell you this. Four years' start would be worth £500 at least; and I find there are no lots now, which have not been granted to the different railways, within a reason-able distance of markets. Another fellow wants to sell half his lot, 320 acres, with improvements, for $4,000, which is the current price of land here now, in fact what some has actually been sold for. But to return: $2,500 — half now, half this time next year, i.e. £260 on the 1st of April, 1882, £260 on the 1st of April, 1883, without interest. The property here increases in value monthly, on account of the railways coming through; and all the lots were handed over to the railway the week before last, I hear, and they are going to charge $5 an acre. It seems to me a pity to go far west, if it possibly can be helped, *when the land can be got safely here, with the value rapidly increasing. Now, is it possible to borrow £500 at 6 per cent. and give the deed as security with leave to recover it when the money is paid in full, plus the interest from date of borrowing — interest paid half yearly? Now, the deed is, of course, more than security, as the value of land always increases. I should be able to put in crops enough to pay the interest and my second half-year's living, thus making the business pay the first half year, having the advantage of another man's four years' work. The man is about to marry, if he can sell out, for the wife won't come up to Manitoba. Directly I heard of this extraordinary bargain I told Boulton, who merely said, "The man always was a fool," and also said that the land is as good as any he has seen. He helped to get off the crops, this year, and saw the place thoroughly, and advises me to buy it, if I can possibly raise the money; he also added that if he had the money he would buy the land for speculation. Now I don't really suppose that I can get enough money, but this will show you, and give you an instance, how a settler can turn over money and double it, with money at his disposal to pick up a chance at the right time. The settlers here range from English gentlemen to common labourers; all nations, sects and classes. Write and tell me your plans as regards myself, as soon as possible. If you don't wish me to start on my own account just yet, I shall employ my time from spring outwards at some trade, in a town such as Winnipeg,* where wages are high; since one can't get steady wages on a farm out here, as nobody has enough money to hire men, even if they had enough steady employment for a man to work at. I have now spent a year and a half at farming, and I feel sure I could pull for myself. I am afraid you will find this letter rather unamusing, but I hope you will reflect on what I have said. I meant to have put in some news of my daily life, but it is ten o'clock, and I must go to bed, my only time for writing being after tea. Mail goes to-morrow. I am very anxious to hear about Aunt Mabel, and I have not had a letter for two weeks; they are forwarded from Eastwood to Bob, then he reads them, and forwards them. I hope, dear mother, you are recovering your late fatigue, for I know it is no light work planning for a lot of thoughtless boys. Some day I hope you will stand at the door of my house, with the stock wandering harmlessly round you, and the yellow grain, glistening in the morning sun, bending in the light breeze. What a happy visit it would be! Always remember me, dear mother.

To his Mother

Cyprus Lodge, December 29, 1881. — *I got your letter of November 21st before those of the 3rd and 12th, owing to Bob's slowness in forwarding them. I am in the very best spot of land in all Manitoba. Land is running up like wildfire. The man whom I spoke about in my last letter has withdrawn his land from the market. If I* get lot 9, I hope to start a grain-wharf close to the station, and buy up all the grain round. I am not working for wages, but for board. Work in winter is scarce, and what there is, is very unpleasant, such as driving the mail, steaming across prairie, and so forth. One takes three or four years to get thoroughly toughened into being out, doing odd jobs, in all weathers, with no one to mend one's things, when one gets in, in the evening. No farmer has enough work to require hiring for more than two weeks in hay, and in harvest; and then, as I said in my last, they change work. I should like to buy a whole lot if possible, with a view to mixed farming, i.e. wheat and stock. I could manage all my stock myself for eight months in the year, and I could then afford to keep a man to help me the other four, in breaking new land, haying, harvest, and ploughing. But, of course, I cannot possibly tell you my plans till I have an idea of the foundation I am to build on. The above is what I should like. The first year I should have to live on money; the second year would just perhaps pay my grub, but no more, the third year would pay my grub and taxes, and the year's allowance of what my farm costs. Here it is as near as I can come to it, first year.

Household effects, stove, blankets, plates, etc.	$75
Tools, pails, etc.	50
Waggon, Bob sleigh and apparatus for same	110
Living	150
Oxen, team	130

Cow and two pigs	35
Fine flooring, window frames, etc., for house	75
Taxes, and cost of land	210
Ploughs and harrows	35
	$870
	or £173 10s.
And supposing I hired 25 acres, broken at $4 an acre	£200
	£193 10

So it would cost £200 to start. The second year one has to buy a team of horses for about $250, and also his cattle. He buys a little more stock according to his means, and probably a mower and reapers and other implements that are necessary. In fact, the more capital one has the more quickly one can make money, and a few hundred dollars' capital will be very apparent in a sensible man's income in three years. Of course I should like *to start in the spring if possible, but if not I can put it off for a year and go further west, because the tide of emigration is enormous now, every train bringing crowds up to Winnipeg; and if I can get land tolerably cheap and near a railway, and in a civilized part, it will be an immense advantage. Every acre of land along the river was taken up by the half-breeds, long before this emigration was thought of; and the land along the* CPR *is all in the hands of speculators, who charge enormous prices, and get it. I don't think I can do better, as far as I can hear from fellows who have been land-hunting this summer, and from surveyors. They say the Saskatchewan valley* is nothing compared with the Red River valley (this part of Manitoba). My plans are stock-raising, and wheat-growing for a certain time. My land will be increasing tenfold all the time, and then, when I am older and wiser and see a good opening, I can sell out and start it. But a fellow cannot farm and do something else, the seasons are too short. If I don't start this year I shall hire out the end of March, either shingle-packing in a mill, or some other steady employment, which one cannot get farming. So much for plans. Now for news. Aunts Mabel and Emma sent me £5, a most useful present: the duty on anything else is thirty-five per cent., and the carriage from Toronto to Beaconsfield enormous, some-thing like £3 for a small parcel by express. The £5 was accompanied by a very kind letter from each. Your letter, a little time ago, about _____frightened me. It reminded me of the time I went to see dear Aunt May's grave with her, and I could not push back the thought however much I tried, the whole scene coming upon me every time. I always keep the little locket on my chain, and when I get tired or angry when working, directly I look at it I always feel better; somehow it seems to have a soothing effect on me and to give me energy. I got father's money, too, and now I wish I had trusted to luck and not asked for any more. I am sadly in want of moccasins and mitts, so this money will come in handy next time I hear of anybody going to St. Leon, twelve miles off, the nearest shop of any kind. We kept Christmas here on Saturday evening, but being "Plym's" there was not much "merry" about it. Prairie chicken pie, plum pudding, and candies.

Extract from diary, December 25th. — *Got up at eight. Fed the horses, and had breakfast. Then Mrs. and Miss Boulton drove off with a neighbour to distribute their Christmas presents. Boulton and I cleaned out the stable, fed the pigs and cows, and watered the live-stock. Washed up the breakfast things. Read a book. Mrs. and Miss Boulton got back at one. Had some Johnny cake and syrup, and cold plum pudding. Read a book. Chopped firewood till four. Watered, fed, and housed the live-stock. Ten, Bible reading and prayers. As a rule we are in the bush almost all day. We get up at 5.30, light the fire, feed the horses and pigs, and clean out the stables. Breakfast, chop firewood for the day, and water the livestock, then start for the bush. Boulton takes his dinner with him. I come back for dinner to feed and water the animals; then I go back to the bush till 4.30. We come back, water the cattle and feed them, and chop some more fire-wood. Tea, letters, etc. Bed at about 9.30. We are getting out logs for a new stable, and have just completed a contract for a bridge. To-day the thermometer has not been above zero, the whole day. This is what I did: Got up at 5.30. Fed the horses and pigs. Breakfast at six. Then put the bridle on Indian pony, and took a pair of whipple-trees four miles to be mended. The drifts were deep in some places after yesterday's storm, and the wind was blowing across the open like anything. My eyes were the only part of my body uncovered.*

107

By-the-bye, could you send me some woollen socks by post? We have to wear three pairs at a time under our moccasins. Costume: fur cap; woollen comforter round my head, mouth, and nose; ditto round my neck; coat, woollen jersey, knitted waistcoat, cloth waistcoat, flannel shirt and under jersey; three pairs of mitts, one under the other; cloth trousers, and woollen drawers; three pairs of socks, moccasins, gaiters. When I am working I gradually strip, as I get warmer; and directly I have done, I pile the whole lot on again. A Manitoba bed is on the same plan. Straw tick, and on that seven blankets (not sheets). If it is very cold, one sleeps between the sixth and seventh blanket; not so cold, between fifth and sixth, and so on. We are short of bedding in this house, as I am an extra; and I have no bedstead, but sleep on the floor. Straw tick and blanket under me; and over me, blanket, quilt, and buffalo robe. One has to sleep with one's head completely covered, or one's nose freezes on a cold night. I could not do it at first, but when I woke I always found myself buried underneath the blankets. Instinct, I suppose.

Well, I was telling you what I did to-day. Got back at 9.30, got the team out and went to the bush. Boulton had gone after finishing the chaws. We shielded up twenty-five logs, which we had cut down before, and brought home a load to build a granary — which requires sixty logs, ten on each side (twenty-two feet long), and twenty rafters. Fed and watered the animals. Dinner. Then Boulton went down to the bush, to draw up the rest of the logs we shielded this morning. A shielding is two logs resting on the ground, with others placed upon them, ready to put on the sleigh. I cut some firewood, then went down to the bridge we were building, and spotted down some of the covering. Nothing in this country has any iron about it; everything is done with poplar, pegged together with oak, and worked entirely with the axe. I am getting so used to the axe now, that I can hew poplar so level that you would almost think it had been planed. But of course I am using the axe almost the whole day, and I had a good deal of practice last winter in the bush. I finished the bridge by 5.30. Moonlight night. Came up, cut some more firewood, fed the animals and watered them. Tea, and then wrote letters. Yesterday was one of those days known in Manitoba as "stormy days." Thermometer 20°, blowing a gale, snow drifting so that you can't see anything. It is the first of its kind I have seen. We only did just what was absolutely necessary out of doors, and were heartily glad to get in again. I cooked the dinner. Boulton is tired of "baching" it, and would have nothing to do with cooking it; and Mrs. and Miss Boulton were writing letters, so I volunteered for the practice of doing it. Well, I fried the ham, and boiled the potatoes, and made a splendid treacle pudding, and baked it, and everyone allowed it was a success. The top was ornamented with the highest art. Next stormy day I am going to bake. I know how to theoretically. Yeast we make out of the wild hops. A servant is a thing not to be got further west than Winnipeg. Land by the Rocky Mountains is $1 an acre, Government obliging every settler to have twenty head of cattle on every hundred acres. I think one gets the land at a nominal rate really. A cousin of Toronto friends have 100,000 acres up there, and is starting a large ranch, and they advised me to go up there. In fact, if I don't settle in the spring, I have a good mind to get into some cattle-party, and work my way up there, and have a look at it, as wages are good up there. Time flies; this time twenty-seven hours we shall be in 1882, and it seems only yesterday it was going to be 1881. This year with all its changes has flown, bringing its petty cares and joys, and leaving no trace behind it. I started this year with $4 in my pocket, I shall start next year with $49, and if it would only increase every year in that proportion, I should soon be rich! Where shall I be this time next year? and what shall I be doing? How many people ask themselves that question every New Year's eve! Now I must say good-bye. Love to all.

To his Mother

Cyprus Lodge, January 5, 1882. — *I am afraid I must write rather shortly this evening, as I owe two or three letters, and time is scarce. I got your letter of December 11th, last mail. The chief point in that letter is settling in the spring. Now I will tell you what are my final plans. By the time you get this, I shall (I hope)* have got a homestead close to here 160 acres. It costs merely the registration fee of $10 (£2). When I am certain of that, I shall pay my board, and immediately begin cutting logs for house, stables, and granary, and lumber, and rails for fencing. I have enough money to do this for the present, i.e., till you get this letter, since I have £5 of father's, and £5 of Aunt Mabel and Emma's; and directly Lot 9 comes into the market, I shall buy it up at $2½ an acre, at six per cent., with ten years to pay it in, in half-yearly instalments. If I can pay for it at the end of first year, all the better. I shall farm my homestead for the necessary three years, at the same time, putting buildings and breaking land on No. 9. By that time I shall thoroughly understand my work. I shall be able to sell my homestead for about $3,000 and get a thorough start on No. 9. If I can have £300 in March to start on, it will be plenty (if judiciously spent) for the first start, i.e. two years. I hope when I am older and wiser, to go in for buying up grain when the steamers run into Hudson's Bay, which they will do when the trade in the north-west makes it worth their while. No land has started to rise with better prospects than this. The greatest wheat-growing and stock-grazing country in the world, it will be. No better climate, no better soil, can be found on the space of the earth, combined with so many natural advantages. Plough the land up, and you have a garden richly manured, to grow whatever you want. Every kind of fruit, almost, grows wild. Beautiful hay for the trouble *of cutting and carting. Dig nine feet into the ground, and you have your well of spring water. No stumps, roots, or stone to break your machinery. The only drawback is that the seasons are unequally divided. Days too short in winter, too long in summer — winter too long, summer too short. This is the only one objection the most prejudiced person can bring against this magnificent country. Of course the winter is cold — no doubt of it. I have got the nail off my finger on account of the frost. Both my ears have been frozen, and on a cold day my nose freezes as fast as I can rub the frost out of it, in the open; but then I am working almost all the time in the bush, where it is as warm as toast, and, as you know, my circulation is like father's, very slow, but when once I do get my blood going, I can gradually slip off coat, and waistcoat, and mitts, and work bare arms; which other people could not do. I was thinking what a grand idea it would be if you were out here: with your knack of turning pence into pounds, and your rich ideas, we should coin money. But I do not think a mill would answer. I am sick of the thought. The grain here is often not properly dried, and spoils the stones and clogs the smutter; besides, I know nothing of milling, and Manitoba is crowded with mills now.... Energy and perseverance, patience and determination, steadfastness and regularity, fair and square and above board, makes the model emigrant. Small beginnings and large endings. I want to begin slowly and surely, and not take one foot up till*

I get the other down. Mill! opposition may kill you at one blow! It costs a large amount to bring it from Ontario, and if it fails I am a ruined man, or rather boy. If my money is in land and improvements, it can't run away; every day's work I put into it makes it more valuable, and my money is safe. Then when I am twenty-five or so, and am sharper and wiser and more keen sighted, if I see a better investment, I can sell out and go in for it. So if you can send me £300, as soon as possible, I will be working in the mean time, to have everything ready to start at once. The snow clears, and "Time is money." I have been doubly losing for a long time, both time and money.* The best way to send out money, is a draft payable to my order, in Winnipeg, on the Bank of Montreal; it has an agency in London, which it would be easy to find out, as it is the Government bank in Canada. I will write to Uncle Shadworth on Sunday, I only hope that I shall some day be able to give some substantial proof that he has not thrown his money away. I have written to the land-agent to apply for the homestead. It was taken up last year by another man, but he has not come up again since, so I may get it without trouble, if he gave it up to the land-office again; if he did not, I shall have to "jump-it," — that is, take two witnesses down to Nelsonville, forty-six miles, where the land-office is, to swear that he has not been

*In his school-days.

113

on for six months, and that he has made no improvements in it. Neither of which he has done. It is a good quarter section, and will do well to start on. A notice will be up in the land-office for one month, asking whether fit cause or reason can be shown why he has done neither; and then I shall have the papers. This man's brother is on the next lot, and that is why nobody has taken it; now he is down below in Ontario. I am afraid my other letters will not be written, as it is very late now — that is, for a farmer. I have seen the thermometer 15° and 54° the same day. The lowest since I have been here is 33° below zero; but the most annoying weather is between 20° and 30° as the snow is two feet deep, melts on one's clothes, and makes one wet through; cracks one's hands badly. Now I must say good-night. Tell Everard, Frank, and Peg, to write. I will write to them when I can, but my only spare time is after tea, and that is chiefly taken up, mending my mitts and moccasins, which is a necessity.

To his Mother

Cyprus Lodge, January 15, 1882. — I am just out of bed after one of those horrible abscesses, which I had just before I left England. It came on from riding barebacked. One can't ride with a saddle in this country, it is too cold. And I had to ride to the blacksmith's, a distance of four miles, to get some whippletrees mounted with iron for the day's work, so I jumped on to the Indian *pony directly after breakfast, at 6.30, one very cold morning, and rode off at full gallop, as merry as a king, little dreaming what I should have to pay for it. I have been in bed just a week; the abscess, from its situation, causing at times terrible pain; it was an enormous one, and I really don't know what I should have done if it had not been for the unexampled kindness of Mrs. Boulton. I shall in future be more careful. Fortunately, Boulton had cultivated some flax this year, so he brought some into the house and thrashed it out, which, mixed with bran, made a good poultice. Mrs. Boulton washed and dressed the place for me herself — always, and read to me in the day, which was so kind. But the nights were the worst parts, as in no way could I lie comfortably, as the weight of the blankets always pressed upon the sore, and made it throb horribly. However, I am convalescent and as happy as a king again, though very weak. My blood must have been in a very bad state, and I wish I had given myself a good dose of something before I came up. I was treated with belladonna at first, to try and put it back; then, when it was found that it was too far advanced, I was given sulphur to bring it to a head, and now I am taking china to strengthen me. Homoepathy has certainly done me a great deal of good, and I hope this is the last of illness I shall have for some time, as I have had a boil somewhere almost ever since I have been here. But the abscess was so enormous, I think it will settle matters for a time. Now, having done* *with the history of my woes, I will tell you something else. Mrs. Boulton has done me a great deal of good in other ways. The beautiful simplicity of her faith, the stories she has read, and the Bible reading every evening after tea, with the accompanying conversation on the same, have, I hope, done me much good too. And it is a great change after France, etc. In my sleepless nights I also thought of my future. And I want to know what you think of this as an immediate plan. I myself want a lot, besides my own homestead, so that when I sell my homestead, I shall be throughly fit to work on a larger share till I find employment on a larger and grander scale altogether, which time and events will show. My own land will therefore be 160 + 640 = 800 acres. The 160 acres I get for $10, the registration fee; 640 I get for $2½ an acre: which makes $1,600 = £330. Now for the other addition. Supposing I buy another lot, which for convenience we will call "Harry's lot," it will cost £330. Now, listen; Harry won't be going to school for three years. One hundred and sixty acres improved — that is a house and, say, twenty acres cleared — is worth $2,000 = £400. The land does not count so much as the improvement. Now, suppose you want £800 for Harry's education. In three years I shall get the deed of my homestead. I shall sell it and go into my other lot, having got my buildings up in the meantime, and get for it £400. The two other lots will cost £660 besides taxes, which comes to $1 a lot per annum. So if you give me £700 down* to buy these lots at once, one for Harry and one for myself, I will buy them up before they are taken. With Uncle S_____'s £300 I shall have enough money to go on with, on my own homestead, for two years at least, and another £100 the third year will buy the necessary machinery for the crops of the improved land and increasing work I shall naturally have to do, which will make the sum total for the three years, £1,060–£660 for the two lots, £300 for farming expenses, £100 for machinery. Now, in the course of the next three years I should be able to get at least one of Harry's quarter lots improved, besides my own work, which makes $200; now I take $800, say for expenses incurred in improving this quarter, and send you $1,200 for Harry's first year and a half's schooling. Thus I am paid for my work, and Harry reaps the profit of his lot. I would improve the other quarter lots as required, or have it done — whichever pays best. Anyhow, I shall always have time in winter to build the houses for them, and do the over-ground work; and it would pay me well, and give ample returns for money expended. Only if you wish me to do this, you must send the money as soon as possible, as speculation in land in Manitoba is past imagination. These calculations are based on present prices, and I am morally certain (as every one else is) that land will be far above these prices in a very short period. The Government has already raised its prices $1 an acre. So now you have my great plan, which will give me a pleasure in the performance, ample remuneration, and Harry as good a dousing of Latin grammar as he can possibly wish for. This is the final plan on which I build my hopes. To-day, being convalescent, and not good for too heavy a strain all at once, I drove Miss Boulton to see a friend about some business. Conveyance, Indian pony and jumper. Jumper is a vehicle made by the settler himself, with no iron about it except at the bottom of the runners. Trails in Manitoba are the tracks in the snow made by traffic, which tracks are filled in as soon as beaten down till trail and snow are one height; but the trail is solid, while the snow all round is comparatively soft under-neath the top crust. Well! going, we slid off the trail, on account of the pony shying, and of course capsized in hopeless confusion of buffalo robes, mufflers, etc. However, we did not suffer any hurt; only it seemed so absurd, calmly reposing in two feet and a half of snow. Coming back, I said I was certain the pony could get under a clothesline which a bachelor settler had hung from his house to his stable. The pony is nervous, and one of the clothes touched his ear. Away we went, slid the trail again, scattering robes, rugs, and Miss Boulton broad-cast, and leaving me triumphant in the jumper. When I drove back to pick up the bits, the tears were running down my cheeks with laughter, I could not speak, much less apologize. Miss Boulton could not laugh — I did not expect her to; but she was not angry. I yelled with laughter the whole way home. Miss Boulton could not see the joke. "All's well that ends well." Best love to all.

To his Mother

Cyprus Lodge, February 3, 1882. — *I received your letter wishing me happy returns of my birthday which shot me effectually out of my "teens." I received the £50 all right, and would have written to mention its safe arrival, but no one went down to the mail. Since I wrote last, I have been down to Nelsonville. I forget how much of the surveying of Manitoba I have told you, so I will tell you the whole now, and you will be better able to understand. Here is a blank map of Manitoba. Each of these squares is 6 x 6 = 36 square miles, and is called a township. Lines running east and west are town-lines, north and south are ranges. I live in 6-9, i.e. town-line 6, range 9. There are eighteen ranges in Manitoba, fourteen town-lines, so you can tell exactly how big Manitoba is. Twelve townships make a municipality, and about six municipalities are electoral districts. Each township is divided into square miles thus, and is called a lot. Boulton's lot is 17. Until three years go a settler could take up any lot he liked, now he can only home- stead even sections. He has a right to homestead 160 acres (a quarter of a section), and to pre-empt 160 more, payable when he gets his deed, $2 an acre. The odd sections in this township are saved for the railway com- pany which runs through, and they are in most other townships, except in four sections, two being saved as "school lots" for a fund for schools, and two for the "Hudson Bay Company," to whom the whole of the*

119

north-west used to belong for hunting and trapping furs. The odd sections, according to the New Land Act of 1882, must be paid for, ready-money. I don't know how much they will cost when they are for sale. They were all for sale, $2 an acre, till last October; but that has been changed. Now to business. A certain man homesteaded and pre-empted the west half of No. 22 in May, 1879, and he has not been on it since, and has made no improvements, contrary to the Homestead Act, which provides that every man should live on his homestead six months in every year; that he shall build a house 18 x 22; that he break fifteen acres per 160. So I accordingly jumped the aforesaid 320; in other words, applied that his homestead should be cancelled in my favour. I hired a team, and two witnesses to swear that he had not been on it, or made improvements, and started for Nelsonville, where the land-office is, forty-five miles from here. Had an affidavit drawn up. A notice was then put up in the office, and also sent to the man, to say that if he did not offer a satisfactory explanation at this office one month from date, his homestead would be cancelled. If he sends an explanation it will be forwarded to Ottawa; so I shall not know for two months at earliest whether I get the lot or not. I had to deposit $20 as a sign of good faith to the Government. I could buy the east half of No. 21, with house, stables, and twenty acres broken, for something under $2,000, which would make a complete section.

Land is rising, and there is a regular fever in Ontario for Manitoba land.... I froze my feet, by foolishly wearing boots on a cold day, and the nails of my big toes are off, after horrible gatherings, the whole way along, which make me waddle rather more awkwardly than a Chinese lady, when I am at work. We had what would have been a blizzard on the prairie to-day. We are sheltered by the bush. It was a clear, nice morning when we went to work, but the wind got up, and the snow drifted so badly that we had to leave our load of rails, and make the best of our way home, with the horses. We went to look at them this evening, and nothing is to be seen but a pile of snow, which means a good deal of digging to-morrow morning. The average depth of the snow is three feet now, though in some places where there is underwood it is drifted seven and eight feet, but after the first sharp spell it gets so hard that a person can walk on the top, though tramping trails for the horses to go along is no joke. However, this only is but once in a winter probably, since it can only happen when a heavy fall of snow is directly followed by a very high wind, which is of extremely rare occurrence in winter. To-day is the first time Boulton has seen it in Manitoba as bad as this. I always cook the break-fast now — porridge or pancakes, fried pork and potatoes; so I shall be ready to bach it on my own account.... Good-night.

Cyprus Lodge, February 12th. — *So that there may be no mistake or misunderstanding, I will again give you my plans, which I hope I made plain in my last letter. As to possibilities, I hope to get the north half of No. 22, but of course I shall not know just yet. If you send me the money, I want to buy the north half of No. 21 from its possessor, for something under £400, all told, including deed, oxen, carts, crops, stove, shanty and stables, and plough. Whether I get his oxen or not, I don't quite know; he does not want to sell them, as he wishes to keep them to go west with. However, that is not a matter of great importance, as they are very unruly, and I do not think I should be able to do much work with them. If I put in eight acres of oats, I should have enough to keep a team, if I can get one cheap in the fall of the year, and then I should have them to draw out my logs and do my winter work with, and of that I shall have plenty to do if I get the north half of 22 also. I shall have to cut out logs for house and stable, and rails to fence in the breaking. I hope Frank will come out this time two years. I think he would be exactly fitted for it, and I am certain he and I should get on together, and I also believe we should mutually benefit each other, in more ways than one. The only stumper in my plans is, who is going to keep house? It is an enormous drawback to a fellow to waste time over cooking meals. Besides, loitering round the stove cooking makes one lazy and*

122

disinclined to work. So all bachelors, as were and as are, say; and I quite believe them. I think I will write to a fellow next fall, if he is still at the college, and ask him to come up. The snow is over two feet now, and getting about is difficult. So I effected a trade with an Indian: I tendered the revolver Aunt Fanny gave me, for a pair of snow-shoes; they are worth about $5. I am not of a blood-thirsty nature, so I did not want the revolver, and I thought Aunt Fanny would not mind my trading it off for something more useful. So please tell her that I regard the snow-shoes as her present, and remember her every time I go down to the mail. One mile without snow-shoes really seems quite four miles, the walking is so terribly fatiguing, whilst one can run along on snow-shoes easier and more comfortably than on bare ground. They are six feet six inches long, and about fifteen inches broad, and when one comes to rough ground where there is no snow, one can slip them off as easily as slippers. They are made of ash with catgut string, a raw hide, and last a lifetime. I bought a rifle for $9, which cost at a store $25 and had never been used; and I had a shot at a wolf at three hundred yards, but missed it, as the wind was too strong. About the north half of 21. The bargain is only till seeding, i.e. the middle of April; so if I can have the money now, of course I should like it, as I could start at once. I must finish now. Love to all.

To his Mother

Cyprus Lodge, February 20, 1882. — .... *Now as to immediate plans. I have given* $10 *as security that I will buy the half section for* $1,800 *(£370), with walls of house, granary and stables, twenty-two acres broken; which is cheap at current prices. Boulton has sold out,* $6,500 *(exclusive of rolling stock — a good deal of which I hope to buy at two-thirds the price, if you send the money before the 1st of April). So I shall have a crop starting, and I hope about* $400 *of grain. I have written to* _____ *offering to pay his passage up, and give him* $10 *a month during the summer months, and his board during the winter. Boulton goes west with the spring. Everybody here has sold out to an English insurance company speculating. They are giving* $8 *to* $10 *an acre for dead land. I should not have been able to get the land I am buying, for less than* $3,200; *but the fellow can't get his deed, as he has never lived on his place. So he will abandon it to me for* $1,800, *and I shall homestead and pre-empt, as if it had never been taken up, which will make no difference to me, as I shall live three years in it at least. The place I jumped, I did not get — bad luck of it. The land-agent, as I thought, had been heavily bribed; and so "worked" the thing for the other man. However, I shall get my security money back, so I only lose my expenses to Nelsonville. I shall buy Boulton's team, a couple of mares, one in foal; also three of his heifers, all in calf; and I have already bought two pigs, and a lot of lumber to finish the house and buildings in the spring before seeding — so you see I mean business. I hope I am not walking on air in all this. It is too good a chance to let slip, and so I hope the money, £500, will be forthcoming by April. The following is an estimate of the probable cost of starting.*

	Dollars
Land, 360 acres	1,800
Seed for crop	60
Team and furnishings-out for summer	325
Sleigh	30
Waggon	40
Ploughs, breaking and stubble	30
Harrows	12
Mower	80
Hay-rake	45
Cow, heifer, and seven calves	180
Finishing buildings	110
Material for same	145
Hired labour	20
House furniture, stove, bedding	50
Tools	25
Groceries, etc.	20
	$2,972

— which is close on £600. The deed of sale for the land is made out for the 8th of April, at which time at least $1,000 must be paid down, and if possible all. If I can get the money over, I want to buy some town lots in Torquay, eight miles from here. I hope to have got the

lot of land before you receive this, on a joint note, as Boulton offers to back it for me. I am doing all this I hope with your concurrence, though I still feel a little nervous about the money being forthcoming at the required date. I think you can trust me, mother dear, to look after my own interests pretty keenly, and get the full value for any money entrusted to my charge.

To his Mother

Cyprus Lodge, March 1, 1882. — *It is hopeless: this chopping and changing about will presently drive me mad. (1) Morpeth Place, N½, 22, 6, 9. He came up and claimed his place within the month; and of course he bribed the agent, or he would never have got it, after two years' absence, when six months is the outside of Government leave. (2) H_____'s place, N½, 21,6,7. The man went back on me, because he was in a hurry to get away, and the fellow who bought it would be able to get his deed for him, which I could not, as I am not "in the ring." (3) Another place. I got out a deed of sale with affidavit duly attested, registered, and sworn, giving him $50 as deposit. Now for the circumstances thereof. This man, to begin with, is a very good fellow, simple and honest as the daylight, and proud. His mother, an English lady, died at his birth; his father, a Canadian farmer, rich, but unkind, put him to work on a farm at ten years old, and never educated him. He would not send him any money to buy a team or finish off his house. The* man waited a month, and then gave up in despair and offered the place to me for $1,800. It is far the best half section round here, W½, 26, 6, 9. We drew up the deed on the printed form, and got it sworn before the commissioners on Tuesday, and I was in high glee. On Wednesday I rode over for the mail. Got your two letters, 20th and 28th, and two for him, — one from his father, saying his uncle was dead, and left him $2,000, and adding that he (his father) had bought him a team, and was just shipping it, and also enclosing a cheque for $500 to finish his house with. I knew by instinct what the letter contained directly I got it at the mail. The poor fellow was terribly cut up, but too proud to ask it back; but of course I could do nothing but insist on his taking it. So, you see, here is casualty No. 3. Bad luck to the whole business! There is nothing for it now but to go west, buy a pair of Indian ponies which can live without oats, a long buckboard, tent, tools and provisions for six months, and "get" directly the snow goes off. My foot is still too bad to think of getting a boot on, and all the flesh is off the great toe down to the bone, and the nail has only just started to grow again, which is a drawback. An entirely revised code of land laws comes out, at the termination of this session, which I am anxiously waiting for. There is no land to be got for a circuit of two hundred miles round here. So much for my sojourn here. The land fever is raging round here still — some land going for $12 and $15 dollars an acre. Boulton returns from

Winnipeg next Saturday, so I shall hear from him the best place to go, etc., besides having to go to Winnipeg myself to buy necessaries. It keeps a fellow on the hop to look for new chances, as quick as the old ones fall through. I don't feel quite so confident as I did, but I know I can stand the roughing all right morally, if I can get through physically. Love to all.

To his Mother

Cyprus Lodge, March 15, 1882. — *You will no doubt wonder why I have not written before this. The reason is simply there was no mail to carry the letters if I had written. Storms and drifting snow have rendered traffic impossible for the last three weeks, but the roads have been broken now once more. I have received your letter to-day of the — I don't know what date, as I have thrown away the envelope, and you don't always date your letters; it is the one mentioning the £600, part of which you say has been sent, and the other is to follow immediately. I will show you that not one penny has been misspent. My farm consists of 360 acres, which has cost me $2,150, and I have already been offered $500 on my bargain twice, but of course refused at once. My reasons for taking up land here are simple: I think I can do better on an improved farm than on the rough grounds, and land is going up rapidly in Manitoba. There is not an acre unsettled now, the papers say. I enclose my letter of the 1st of March, which I got out of the post-office*

on account of the stoppage of the mails and my change
of plans. I got the present place by stratagem, and the
aforesaid stratagem cost me the freezing of both my
feet up to the ankles, which took Alfred and Boulton
four hours to rub out, and caused me terrible agony.
This happened twelve days ago, and I can only just walk
now. Cause — wet socks, holes in my shoes, no dinner,
and sixteen miles to walk in heavy snow, and snow-shoes.
I thank God that I ever got home; and I never should if
Boulton had not beaten me every time I stopped, I was
so utterly exhausted. I laugh at the whole thing now,
but I did not whilst my feet were being thawed out.
Carelessness, nothing else, except perhaps a slow circulation. My farm, eighteen acres broken, a house, or rather
shanty, and stable. I shall have to go down below almost
directly, probably to buy a team; they are so expensive
up here, and bad too. It will pay me, as I get the ride
back for nothing, and I don't want to have my horses
dying in the stable, as most of the teams for sale up
here do. Boulton wants $350 for his two mares, one
twelve, the other fifteen years old. I can get a decent
youngish team down below for $225, and it costs $75
to bring them up. I know a party in Ontario, whom I can
depend upon to choose a good team for me, so I shan't
be swindled; and I can't depend on myself entirely, of
course. I got a delightful letter from Eton to-day, a jolly
letter, and so kind. Everard also wrote, short and pithy....
Love to all.

To his Father and Mother

Shore Lake Farm, April 21, 1882. —*I have not written for a month: I plead guilty. I have received the sums, £600, Bank of Montreal, £50, Bank of England notes. I am not going to thank you for the above now, because I cannot; but I shall be back some time in the next four years, and then I will thank you. God grant I may repay you one hundredfold for your kindness to me, by leading a steady and upright life; showing that you have not misplaced your kindness. I will explain why I cannot get more than a certain amount of land. Manitoba is settled up. There is no more homesteading; I bought mine from a private individual. The great aim of the Canadian Government is to prevent speculation; and the laws are so framed that an individual cannot have more than 360 acres in his possession. A colonization company can take up 1,000,000 in D, if it likes, but a single individual can't. Dash made his money in town lots — a species of gambling; in fact I would rather sit down and play a game of Nap, at $5 points, because I might have some idea of what I was doing. I intend to farm steadily for two or three years, then when I am older I may possibly speculate in land a bit. I possess 320 acres, 15 of which are broken. I rent Boulton's place at a nominal cost, 38 acres of which are broken; so I shall have 53 acres in crop.*

Wheat: Boulton's place. — Field across the river, 16 acres; 28 bushels; seed, gold drop. My place. — 9-

acre field; 15 bushels; seed, Scotch pips, red. 4-acre field; 8 ditto.

Oats: Boulton's place. — Field in front of house, 8 acres; 24 bushels, black and white. Field behind house, 10 acres; 30 bushels, black and white.

Barley: My place. — 1 acre; 3 bushels, hulless. Timothy Boulton's place. — 4 acres.

Now this was my line of argument. If I ran my own place alone I should have to do it by myself; it would keep me going pretty briskly, but would not keep an extra man. Now, by running Boulton's place, I can afford to hire a good and experienced man, and whilst keeping him occupied learn myself, as of course I am totally ignorant of breaking, sowing, etc. This summer I hope to build a granary and a house; a shanty and a stable I have already. Possibly I may turn the present stable into a hog-pen, and build another stable instead of a house, — I have not settled yet. It is 9.30 p.m., and I have just been out to give the horses their oats, and see that they are all right before going to bed. Can you picture me all alone, no one nearer than three-quarters of a mile? Cook for myself, bake for myself, wash for myself, and eat my meals, go to bed, get up, all by myself. This is Friday. Next Tuesday, Bob Irving, my hired man, a jolly, hard-working labourer comes; I have known him for the last five months, and have never seen him without a smile upon his face. I expect we shall get through our summer's work in style. I got a nice letter from Frank, and another equally nice from Aunt Emma last mail. By-the-bye, I have never told you why I have not written for so long. I was in Winnipeg for four days, and it took me six days to get there, and six to come back; and every place was so full. I could not get a place to write in away from home. I could not find Palmer. I found a batch of emigrants who knew him, but they did not know where he was lodging. You see that, on account of the storms, no mail either arrived here or left, for three weeks; indeed, we had only one mail for five weeks: the roads were blocked up with drifts, so I did not get your letter till Palmer had been in Winnipeg a week, so I could not catch him. He must have been out at a farm twelve miles from here. I hired a horse and cutter, and after great difficulties got six miles: the snow was so soft that the horse sunk down to its belly (a vulgar but proper term) every step it took, so I had to give it up, and come back. I thank you very much for sending out the things; I only hope I shall get them all right. I enclose a letter I wrote a month ago, but on account of the irregularity of the post never finished. I was obliged to put Cannon off when I hired Boulton's place and a skilled labourer: I wrote with many apologies. I think I can do what carpentering I want myself, as I remember something of my carpentering at Haileybury, — "and something of your bad writing, too," you will say; but I am in a hurry, and I want to get to bed, as I have to start to Norquay early to-morrow with a grist. It was snowing for a change to-day. I hope to start seeding on Wednesday next, if I have luck, and then my letters will be short and sweet, as I shall be on the hop till next November. Indeed, I have been hopping pretty lively for the last week, because when one has to do all the indoor work as well, one has not much time to meditate on the changes and chances of life. I want to break twenty acres, and hire twenty acres broken this summer; and then I can afford to have a hired man again. Bob, I hope, will stay with me till this time next year, if he comes. He will learn just as much with me as with an ordinary farmer; I don't mean to say he will learn from me, but from what he sees done on my place. I only hope he will earn his board, as living is terribly expensive now; pork, eighteen cents per pound, which very soon makes a hole in a man's pocket. Now I must go to bed. With love to all.

To his Mother

Shore Lake Farm, May 18, 1882. — *It is a month since I wrote, and now I am scribbling in a hurry, and as fast as possible, to let you know how I am getting on, before I go to bed. I think I have probably got N½, 22, for a homestead and pre-emption. Luck! makes me 640 acres. I bought the other place from a private individual. There is no Government land round here. Might just as well try and take up land round my old home in England! If I do get No. 22, it will be through a combination of consummate cheek (a thing a fellow must* have in this country) and luck. I got a letter from Mills, saying Bob was working at Southwood, Ontario, and returning me my money. I wish you would explain to Mrs. Cannon, that when I determined to take Boulton's place it necessitated my having a thoroughly experienced and hard-working man with me, so I could not have her son. I also got a letter from Palmer. He is working near Winnipeg. His luggage has not arrived yet. I also got a letter from Uncle Charlie, enclosing what he called "a trifle," but what I call "a nice little pile." I find I shall have to buy a selfbinding reaper; cost, $320; three years' payment. This summer labour is scarce. I shall have plenty of money to run me on till Christmas, and for another two years, if you like; but if I had money enough to buy another team, I could rent Boulton's place again next year, and by that time I shall have forty-five acres broken on my own place, which would keep them both going. I should go down below at Christmas, and get the team and some good stock (cows and pigs) to bring up with me. I should want £150 in December for that, and I would give you my note at eight per cent. (payable in December, 1883) for it, out of my crops; but we can talk over that between this and Christmas, and you have already done far more for me than I deserve. You would naturally like to overhaul my accounts, so I will make them out, and send them the first time I have a minute to spare. I have not missed a day in my diary, or a cent in my accounts, since January 1, 1881; so I can always tell you what I am doing and spending. The winter of 1884 I hope to spend in England once more. It is a long time to look forward to, but I can't leave my place before then. I shall come home for nothing, as I know one of the large cattle-exporters well, and he offered to give me $15, and intermediate passage back, to take charge of a cargo for him. I shall soon have been out two years, and it seems like a few days, everything rattles past so quickly, —always getting out of and into bed, with no time to look round hardly between. Grandmamma wrote a very nice letter to me, which I must answer by this mail if I can, but it keeps me up so late at night, and then I don't get enough sleep to rest myself thoroughly. I remember the time when I could not get up after ten hours' sleep, and now I roll out of bed directly the alarm sounds five. How father will enjoy his trip out here, if he comes. No worry and bustle, except the bull-dogs and mosquitoes, and they are getting bad now. A little later and we shall get up at three, and lay over in the middle of the day, as the bull-dogs (large flies) worry the horses so much. By-the-bye, if I don't marry before I am thirty-two it will be a miracle. I come in awfully hungry at noon, and by the time I have cooked the dinner over the hot stove, my appetite is gone. Baking, washing, mending, leave no time to write or do anything. It is now 11.30, and I have to be up at 4.30 to-morrow to sow my last four acres of oats before the wind gets up; so I am afraid I must say good-night. The saw and grist

135

mill at Norquay was burnt down in ten minutes last week, and my lumber won't be sawn this summer, I am afraid. I must say good-night.

To his Grandmother

Shore Lake Farm, May 18, 1882. — *Thank you so much for your kind letter and present, although I am afraid the beer is impossible, because there is none nearer than Emerson, 107 miles distant, and it would sour on the way out, since the rainy season is coming on, and this is the worst country in the world for thunderstorms. But my feet are healing rapidly now, and there is no fear till next winter, when I shall have to be very careful with them, to keep them from decaying. I shot a couple of minks the other day, and I have tanned the fur, which I shall sew inside my moccasins, and that I think will keep them all right. I hope you will excuse my not having written before, but twenty-nine acres of wheat and eleven of oats, with one team and two men, and only four months and a half to sow and harvest it, erect fences, and break thirty acres of new land and take the scrub off, besides all the cooking, washing, and mending, does not leave me much time for many things which ought to be done. I have not even found time to find the corner stake of my property yet; and then, you see, I did not complete my purchase till just before seeding, so I am a little behindhand. I have four acres of oats more to sow, and now it is raining, or I would have had them in to-day, so I have been fencing. The mode of fencing is peculiar to this country. There is no wood except poplars round here, and the bush is of two kinds, according to age—rail-timber and logs. The fires which come along in the fall sometimes kill a whole bush. Three years ago a fire came through here and killed a good many, leaping half a mile at a time, burning everything in its way. The way to stop it is by ploughing three furrows ten yards from the object to be saved, and five furrows twenty yards from these, thus arresting its course. The rails are cut fifteen feet long, the pickets seven feet. The pickets are jammed into the ground two feet with the hand, and by pouring a little water in after starting the hole. The pickets are bound together with willow. The rails are put eighteen inches from the ground with a stake. The only objection is that the poplars rot so fast. But when the railroad comes we shall be able to buy cedar posts and put up bushed wire fences, which will of course be much better. The mosquitoes are beginning to sing, and bite too. The grass is getting green, and the dreary-looking poplars are donning their scanty foliage. I am afraid this letter is very "shoppy;" but farming is occupying all my thoughts just now. I will try and write a more interesting letter in the course of the next three weeks. Pray tell Mrs. Blaxter I noticed two or three Hillington postmarks, and mentally thanked her. Give my love, etc.*

To his Uncle

Beaconsfield, May 18, 1882. — *I have just got your letter, which, as you may well imagine, surprised me. "The trifle" you so kindly sent surprised me, because it happened to be exactly the thing I wanted, to carry on my "work" satisfactorily, and for that I cannot thank you enough. But your letter was what surprised me more; it said so much in a few words, and I don't think I ever received a letter before which made me feel so happy as yours did, — the same feeling, I suppose, as a fellow has walking down the "big school" to get the prize at the end of the term. A "cork toe" I hope will not be necessary, as my feet are healing fast. I think I have also got the half section I jumped, in January, which will make my little property two miles long and half a mile broad. I am sorry to say that I cannot write home so regularly now, as I am crowded with work (forty acres in grain), and all the fencing to put up, clothes to wash and mend: all these leave but little time for letter-writing. Up at five. Bob (my hired man) goes out, feeds the horses and pigs, cleans out the stable, and throws the harness on; meanwhile, I get the breakfast. After breakfast, about 6.15, we have a smoke to aid digestion, and wash up the breakfast things, then steady work till noon. I come in a little before, to put the potatoes on to boil, as they take so long, and then we give ourselves and horses an hour and a half's rest, then out again till 6.30 or seven, it depends whether we are pressed* to finish something. Then tea, wash up dishes, mend things, set bread (if required), and then bed, and glad to get to it. On the jump the whole time. All the land within one hundred miles of here, worth taking up, is now under cultivation; and I believe I am in about the best farming part of Manitoba. Floods have been bad in Emerson, everybody living upstairs, water five feet in the streets. The fellow who brought my waggon out from Emerson, had to bring each wheel, axle, etc., over the Red River, separately in a skiff, and it cost him $4, the bridge being washed away by the flood. The prairie round the Mennonites is three feet in water, so I am afraid they will not get much crop in this year. We are in the hills, where no floods can reach us. However, I will not enter into a description of the country, because I hope that when you are tired of the old world for travelling, you will come over and see the new one, and all its novel labour-saving arrangements. I find I can save money by buying a self-binder, i.e. a machine which reaps the grain and binds it into sheaves at the same time, with wire. It will cost me $340, — January 1, 1883, $120; 1884, $120; 1885, $100: but then I shall cut for other people at $2 an acre, and I can cut ten acres a day; wire four pounds to the acre, at eleven cents per pound. Labour is already very scarce round here, and during harvest prices will be terrible, and men will not be able to be got for love or money. I shall be independent of much help, as my man will be able to shock up most *of the grain, and I can give him a hand in the evening, after reaping. I have four more acres of oats to sow. The wheat I have sown looks well, and is coming up nicely. I am a little behindhand, but then I have a large crop for one team to put in, and I have put it in more carefully than most round here, and harrowed it oftener; and besides that, I had so little time to prepare for it before seeding, on account of buying my place later. Good seed had to be picked out and drawn over, implements bought, and one thing and another; so I don't blame myself for being a little behind. The fellows round here are mostly sons of English clergy, and a rough lot at that; the nicest fellows being the common rough "launks," always good-natured and ready to oblige, which the former by no means are. I am sorry to say I have not answered Aunt Mabel or Aunt K.K.'s last letters, but I will as soon as I can. With love to them all, and sincerest thanks to yourself for your extreme kindness.*

I am your very affectionate nephew, — EDWARD

TO HIS MOTHER

Shore Lake Farm, June 29, 1882. — Business, business, business! Going on rapidly. Down to Winnipeg two weeks ago. Saw Palmer, who is getting on well; luggage not arrived yet. I bought another team for the following reason: my present team is not nearly strong enough for the excessively hard work of breaking with a 14-inch plough in scrub, and Jessie has one of the strongest, healthiest, and prettiest bay foals you ever saw. I hope both Jessie and Queenie will have foals next year. Bill and Jack, my new team, are two bright bays, very big and strong, and run along with the 14-inch breaker as if it were a plaything. Our working hours through breaking have been — 3.00 a.m.; breakfast, 3.30 to 9.30, breaking; 9.30 to 10.30, chores and dinner; 10.30 to 4, sleep; 4 to 5.30, tea; chores 5.30 to 10.30, breaking. The reason for this is the bull-dogs (horse-flies, I think, in England) are so thick and annoying, that the horses go nearly mad in the day. The mosquitoes are bad at night, but that can't be helped; last night they were like a cloud of dust, and made a noise like a swarm of bees, into one's nose and ears, and biting like fury. However, the grass is getting long now, so breaking will soon be over. I shall have twenty acres broken — not so much as I intended, but I could not hire anyone. The scrub is too hard for stray comers to get out. As a matter of curiosity, I went, when in Winnipeg, to the chief loan-office, and tried my luck. $4,000 cash was the highest bid for N½, 21; or a $2,000 mortgage, nine per cent. for three, five, or ten years. Now for the reason of this. Ever since I bought this place, which I think is one of the best in Manitoba as regards situation, I intended to put up a saw and grist-mill (portable), but I had not intended putting one up for two years; reasons, lack of cash, and lack of custom. Now, if I can, I will put the saw-mill up at the end of October. People are flocking past my house every day,

141

to take up the rough but well-wooded lands in 6, 11; 7, 8; 7, 9; 7, 10, and all north of me. Now the nearest mills are St. Leon, fourteen miles south. Norquay mill, 8, SW, burnt down with very little hope of building up; so I should get all the trade north of me, and south of the Portage, and for eight miles south-east and west. Now is my chance. People are beginning to shingle (wooden slate) their buildings instead of thatch, and are putting up frame houses instead of log. Go gently. Saw mill before the winter sets in. Hire a good sawyer. Grist-mill, next summer, with the proceeds of the saw-mill. This is the plan I hatched a long time ago, but kept quiet; and this is the scheme I intend to carry out. If you can furnish me with £300 or £400, at seven per cent., payable half-yearly, by October of this year, either on my note of hand, or a mortgage, which you like, I can buy a 15-horse-power engine, and saw-carriage frame and rigging, by paying $1,200 cash, and the rest on my note which I could pay during the winter. There you are. I have made my inquiry quietly, so that no one shall get a hint of what I am at, so, if you can't furnish me with the cash, I shall not have to bear the sneers people are so ready to heap on failure. Crops are looking splendid. My self-binder has arrived, and I have got orders to cut 100 acres at $1 75 cents an acre. The wire costs 50 cents an acre, 12 cents per pound, so I shall be able to pay off my first note with it. I am a little hard up for cash just at present, so I am sending one team out *to Emerson with a load, for which I get 60 cents per 100 lb., and I take 2,500; and for the load I bring back I get $1 35 cents per 100 lb.; and that's how I replenish my purse when it gets temporarily low. Work, and sleep, eat, and work, is the daily routine, on the dead run the whole time; and every now and then I look round and imagine I see a saw- and grist-mill looming up on the hill, at the border of the lake. You will all be coming out to have a look at me and mine some day. I am young and hopeful, but at the same time I think I can look at both sides of the question; and the earlier a man begins, the earlier he wins, and I am afraid someone else will get ahead of me if I don't look sharp; so, my dear mother, as usual I leave it to you. I know you know my weaknesses, but also my strong. points: if I say that $2,000 shall be paid back in full at the end of three or five years, as you like, with seven per cent. in the interval, you know as well as I do that it shall be paid by hook or crook, even if everything went against me, which I don't think is likely. I should add a chopping machine for grain at once if you concur in my views, and hope to have the grist running by next July, and meditate enlisting Palmer's services, as he seems a nice fellow, and his wife is a nice quiet refined woman. Live-stock as follows —*

First team: grey mare, "Jessie" and foal; cream, "Queenie." Two dogs, "Collie" and "Syndicate." Second team: bay, "Jack"; dark bay, "Bill." Setter, "Rover"; one cow, one cat, four sows, two barrows, one thoroughbred boar and one thoroughbred sow. Total 19.

143

Roller, harrows, waggon. Dermont, two ploughs.
McHorrwich's wire-binder. Two bob sleighs, two sets of
harness, farm tools, household furniture, etc.

TO HIS GRANDMOTHER

Beaconsfield Post Office. — *I am afraid it is some*
time since I have written, but I hope you have seen
some of my letters home, and thus know tolerably well
how I am getting on; it is rather hard these busy times
to squeeze in a letter. I suppose the summer climate of
Manitoba is almost unexcelled — at least I know England,
France, Germany, and Ontario cannot compare with it,
— not too hot, and always a wind. But the mosquitoes,
they are indeed terrible in the evening; no rest for man or
beast. We always keep a stove, full of straw and stuff,
burning all night with the pipes off; and I have not come
to any satisfactory conclusion yet, which is best, or rather
worst, the mosquitoes or the smoke. I have had an addi-
tion to my household in the form of a young English-
man, aged sixteen. Poor fellow! he came out to a fellow
near, and could not work hard enough for him; so he went
to another man, and the same thing occurred again, and
the man gave him a day to find new quarters in the
middle of Manitoba! Nobody would have anything to do
with him; I was asked to take him when first he came
in, but refused, knowing he would be more comfortable
where there was a woman. However, he came over to me
in despair, and asked me to drive him to Smart's landing,

to catch the steam-boat for Winnipeg. I found out he only had $8 (£2) in his pocket, so I told him it would cost more than that to get to Winnipeg, besides what he would have to pay for board whilst looking out for office work. He asked me in despair what he was to do: "If I can't work hard enough for one man, I can't for another"; so I told him to go and give my hired man a hand for a couple of hours, and in the meantime I drove to his former place and got all his luggage. I never saw a fellow look so surprised and happy in all my life, as he when I called him in to dinner, and he saw all his luggage stowed away about the house. Poor fellow, he was as happy as a king, and has worked away splendidly ever since, and seems quite happy. He came up this morning and meekly asked whether he might go and bathe. How I laughed. I explained to him that in this country, where wages are so terribly dear, and men so hard to get, that, as he was only working for his board, I did not expect him to consider himself bound to work from six in the morning till eight at night; and considering he has to ride two miles to feed the pigs on my own place, before breakfast at six in the morning, and after supper at seven, I think he does remarkably well, and seems to enjoy it. Haying is the order of the day, and I hope by the time you get this letter we shall have begun harvest. I can boast the best field of wheat in the township, I am glad to say. Last Sunday my best horse died, and none of the magnates of the township can assign any reason except poisonous grass, which has frightened them all very much. It is a great loss to me, and a great disappointment, and it takes off the pleasure of farming considerably. He was a beautiful bay horse, and my favourite; and I am not ashamed to say that my eyes were decidedly moist as I hitched the other team on to draw him away to be food for the wolves. Poor Jack! I bought him cheap, because he was said to be balky — that is, he would not pull when it did not suit him. He was a very powerful horse, and though I had some very heavy loads over rough boggy country, to use a Cannock expression, "He never went back on me"; which convinced me the former teamster had given him a bad name by his own ignorance and bad treatment, and that kindness goes a long way with man and beast. Poor Geoff seems to be in low spirits, and I fear in very poor health; I shall soon be recommending a "year in Manitoba." I had a delightful dream last night. It was Christmas night: all were at the Christmas dinner except Frank and myself, as we were supposed to be toiling in young Beaconsfield. Father got up to propose our health and success — and we walked in, and I woke. I am afraid this letter will be terribly uninteresting to you; but farming, except to farmers, and sometimes even to them, is uninteresting.

I am your affectionate grandson, — EDWARD

TO HIS MOTHER

Beaconsfield, August 17, 1882. — I have just got your two letters of July 22nd and 25th, both of which *are peculiarly interesting in their way. Of course Bob is anti-Manitoba, but if he comes up here I will do my best for him. If I had £20,000 left me to-morrow, I would not leave this place, though farming, of course, is not always enjoyment. My hired man and myself alone have cut with the scythe, among briars, laying logs and dead grass, fifty tons of hay, and that was not exactly enjoyment! Thanks to my parents' kindness, I started half up the ladder, and under peculiarly favourable circumstances, and have every prospect of an exceedingly abundant harvest. My foal is allowed to be the finest in the township; one of my fields of wheat is without exception the thickest I have seen, and the envy and admiration of my neighbours, — Dame Fortune, of course, chiefly; but also because I did not try, like most of my neighbours, to be the first to get my seeding done, but harrowed and rolled my land well. On account of the exceeding drought when it ought to have rained — June, — and the heavy rain when it ought to have been fine — July, — hay is scarce. I had to scour all over my land to get enough, and everybody else is short. I have put up twice as much as I want myself, and hope to get rewarded for my pains to the tune of $12 a ton in the spring. The country is at present hard on horses, bad accommodation, and flies — bull-dogs or horse-flies — and mosquitoes go for them most unmercifully. I think I mentioned in a letter to grandmother the loss of my best horse, which was a great shock to me. Since that, two neighbours* have both lost horses, and another of mine is just recovering. It had a terrible shave. It was on Saturday night the inflammation came on, and although I had just had a kick from a horse, I hopped on to him, and rode or rather drove him to the doctor's five miles off, and just in time. He seems to be recovering pretty well just now. I shall have to go and buy another the day after tomorrow, for harvest, as I cannot use Jessie, who has a foal. The advantage of the wire-binder is, the wire does not break, and the compression on the wire-binder will bind much tighter, which in the case of oats is necessary, since they have to be cut on the green side, and shrink when dry, consequently in the case of string there is very little left when it has passed the various stages and arrived at the thrashing-machine. We expect to begin harvest about the end of next week. Barley is being cut now; but, thank goodness, I did not put any in. Now for the most important part of the letter. I had given up hoping for my mill, and often upbraided myself for asking you, and raising hopes, and so you can fancy the pleasure it gave me, the pleasure that I can be depended on; and you shall not be disappointed, as I hope, by the brains nature gave me and steady work, I shall be able to show, you have not done wrong in placing the money in my hands. I feel in a way responsible to brothers, and sisters, and all, and a very pleasant feeling it is. Of course you will want money some day to bring Helen and Charlotte out, and I shall be able to give Harry a hand in the scholastic

148

course; the pleasure of thinking of all this is worth double the common idea of piling up money for one's self. I have ordered the saw-mill. I hope to have it set up in two months, just before the frost sets in. Shingle and saw-mill complete, 20-horse power; capacity seven thousand feet per day. Prices $8 per thousand for sawing, or take half the logs — which the owner likes; lumber sawn $22 per thousand. Of course, you will all come out some day, and spend a year with me. How they would enjoy the free life! I shall be able to form an idea of how far my plans will be feasible, and how far they may have to be extended or reduced, by the winter, and what means I can get hold of to carry them out with. A railroad, they say, is to pass within three miles of here. I might be able to reduce that to a minimum by showing I could form a village and industries. There is no limit to man's capabilities, as long as he can keep the ball rolling, but that he must do, and keep control of it, as if once it gets beyond his reach, it is difficult to catch it up again. I think we are going to have a tough harvest, as the new moon has set in with a terrible amount of wind, and my binder will show its superiority to the single one-horse binder in one respect anyhow. At present I have a family, consisting of father, son, daughter, and son's wife in my house, and they go near to driving me mad. Airs!! "Never were in such a country." "Never used to this sort of thing," etc., etc. The commonest sort of English labourer, polished by twelve years' residence in Ontario. It makes a sweet *mixture of the most contemptible airs and blow I ever saw — living mostly on me, on the strength of the wife cooking for me, and I could cook three times as well and as fast myself; and, of course, as the housekeeping things are not theirs, they use them freely, to say the least of it! However, I shall be moving over to my place soon, and then they will have notice to quit at short notice. The son is chawing away something like hay, close by me, so unless I stop in time, I might say something irreverent, so I must say good-bye, my dearest mother. My gratitude to you I cannot describe, but you know it without description. Tell Frank to sit down, and write me a letter, not a note; plans, etc., in a comprehensive form.*

To his Aunt

Beaconsfield, September 23, 1882. — *Believing that I had performed all imperative duties, and resting in innocent security, I have thoroughly enjoyed my pipe every evening after tea, and then turned into bed, after thanking God for the bountiful blessings He was bestowed upon me, the magnificent weather He has given, and the abundant harvest, and the splendid health and spirits I at present possess to aid me in securing it. But, I have had my spell of bad luck; and thereby hangs a tale, which only unfolded itself last night, and annoyed other people as well as myself. As mother may have told you, I invested in a self-binder, as the only means of getting my harvest in, since labour is not to be got round here.*

It worked well the first two days, and then a casting broke, on account of a flaw, and I had to go to Norquay to have it mended, or rather to get another casting; and off I started at once, with a light rig and a team, eight o'clock at night, and cold, so I put on my great-coat, a thing I have only worn twice since I have been in the country, since it is too long to walk in. I put my own letters and the letters of three other people in my capacious pockets; among them was a letter to you and a receipt. At Norquay they had not the casting required. Off I started for Nelsonville, in very low spirits, forty-five miles from Norquay to Nelsonville, my crop waiting to be cut, and very hard on the team; it was a very hot day and the roads were very rough. I got to Nelsonville about 7.30 p.m. Had supper, went out to give the horses their oats, and found Bill off his feed. I suppose this, coupled with the shaking on the road and the disappointment of the delay, were too much for me, anyhow I went for a veterinary surgeon, gave my horse some scalded bran, and then fainted on my way from the stable to the hotel, which of course created a delightful bit of excitement for the natives of a little western town. When I came to, I was lying down in the bar-room, with a crowd round me, and the bar tender energetically emptying a bottle of whisky down my throat, which naturally made me more annoyed still. However, I requested to be woke at five, and slept soundly, got up next morning feeling all right, fed my horses and had breakfast, and then began kicking at the machine-agent's door. This did not have the desired effect till eight, and, after all, he had not the casting I wanted. Now Emerson is sixty-seven miles from Nelsonville, and I must go there, and my crop waiting, and half a dozen other crops all wanting cutting. I immediately went to all the stables to find whether there was a horse that could go to Emerson and back in two days; I found one that was guaranteed to do the journey. I promised to take every care of it, and, leaving my team as surety, I started with horse and buggy. I got into Emerson by nine at night of the second day from leaving home; got my casting; my horse ill, went to a veterinary, sat up all night administering the medicine, and then started out at 1 p.m. of the third day; got into Nelsonville after frequent stops, and walking most of the way myself, by nine in the morning of the fourth day. Started out with my own horses, and got home at 8 p.m. of the fourth day, having gone 224 miles in four days; and I was very glad to get home, and my machine was spinning round the field at 6.30 next morning. Now, on Wednesday, I met a neighbour named Woods, and he asked me in rather an indignant manner if I had posted an Ontario letter he gave me. I said, "Yes! of course I did," and thought no more about it, till yesterday, when F_____ W_____ asked me the same question (he is an Englishman who is staying with me). He asked me during dinner, and I remembered Woods's question, and the coincidence struck me as curious, so I went to my great-coat, which had never been touched since it had been thrown out of the waggon, when I got home. There were two newspapers which ought to have been posted, but the letters were all gone. Now, through the muddle, disappointment, and excitement of the last month, I could not and cannot remember anything about the letters, except meaning to post them at Norquay, and then at Nelsonville when I found I had to go there; but whether they dropped out of my pocket or were taken out, and where, I cannot tell. I am more annoyed than I can say, because I feel exceedingly grateful to you, and your mind will naturally run to those black and yellow stockings, as mine did when I pulled out those newspapers. I broke the axle of one of my wheels, crossing from my place to Boulton's afterwards. Luckily, as I only use three horses on the binder, I had one doing nothing in the stable, and he took me to Nelsonville and back, seventy-four miles in twenty-one consecutive hours. In other words, I broke down at 11 a.m. on the Wednesday, and I was running at 9 a.m. on Thursday. Now all my magnificent harvest is cut, the binder is now over my head in pieces, and eight long stacks show what two teams and four men can do in a week's drawing in; three days more stacking and then the plough will be again scraping the ground. I have hitched the contents of fourteen waggon loads on to the stacks to-day, and as a considerable number of the sheaves had to go "scooting" a good distance through the air before they reached the required *altitude, my arms ache and my back aches, and my eyes ache; and yet I say what a glorious life is this, with all its drawbacks. The letter I wrote before was a long one, and I cannot try to tell you more of my plans after these days of martyrdom and slavery. This is an apology for what I hope you will consider an excusable oversight; it is not intended to interest you particularly, or give you news. I have not written home for some time; it is impossible. When man or boy is working through harvest, he seizes every moment of peace as the miser clutches his gold. With my large harvest it is hard work, but in the long winter evenings letters long and happy I hope will come. My saw-mill, thanks to you, is now, I hope, wending its way up to Manitoba. With love to all, I am your very affectionate and grateful nephew, —* EDWARD

P.S. If you happen to be writing home, will you tell mother that an early and comprehensive letter will shortly be on the road. Wheat will average thirty-two bushels per acre, fine sample; oats, fifty-five; barley, none sown. Potatoes, large crop and some bigger than an ordinary turnip, and, for flavour, they are as only Manitoba potatoes can be.

This is the last letter received from the lad, and brings us to the end of his second year in America. Those who have read these simple, straightforward letters can hardly think the results unsatisfactory. A boy of eighteen leaves England, with no experience and no advantages beyond average health and strength, and the courage and determination which are the characteristics of Englishmen. He earns his experience for himself, through considerable hardships certainly, but finding kindness and help always ready to back honest endeavour. He was thus able to avail himself of the first opportunity that seemed to offer a good chance of success, and start on his own account. A small capital here was necessary, and indeed the letters seem to show, that unless a young man can count upon a certain sum of money — not less, we should say, than between £700 and £1,000 being forthcoming when required — an emigrant's life must be hard and success slow. But with £1,000 at his command, the writer of these letters has been able, within two years, to establish himself in a farm of about seven hundred acres, his own property, and a fair proportion of it already under cultivation; he has his house, two teams of horses, cows, pigs, etc., eight stacks of corn, and fifty tons of hay, besides his ploughs, reaping and binding machine, etc. He is now starting a saw-mill, to which grist machinery will be added in the spring, and may fairly look forward to making a really good profit for the next year, with the prospect of continually increasing and developing his business as the country becomes more and more settled. Thus we may hope that his time of real hardship is nearly over, and that he has before him a life of great and varied interest, with every prospect of success from the merely worldly point of view; but not only so. The emigrant's career need not be only a continual hunt after the almighty dollar, everyone for himself, with the devil on the heels of the hindermost. One of the points that struck us most on reading the letters as they came, was the kindness the boy met with from the first day on board the steamer, down to the time he set up for himself. In fact, the obligation he owes, and feels that he owes, to those excellent people at Shore Lake Farm is difficult to calculate. Such people we fear must be rare in a country where the race for money cannot but harden the exteriors of life at all events; but the remembrance of what he owes to the good nature and assistance of friends will, we doubt not, keep him always on the alert to do the same for young fellows starting as he did, in a strange land. And then, so far from his life being one of selfish excitement, we may fairly hope from the tone of these letters that while money-making must be the outward gauge of success, yet the life before him may be as useful, and present as many or more opportunities for the exertion of the finer qualities of manhood, as almost any profession. The feeling of relief we felt on reading each letter as it came, and finding that, so far from hardening the boy's character, the hard work and excitement seemed to develop the better side of his nature, has been our chief inducement to publish them. Surely many a young fellow now hopelessly struggling with his competitive examinations, might with advantage to himself exchange slavery at his crammers for such a life with all its hardships. These letters at all events give a true and unvarnished account of what he would have to expect, and what he might fairly hope for, and, unless we are blinded by our partiality, show that, however hard and uphill may be its course, there is a bright side to the emigrant's life.

THE END

36,200